Come Lean on Me

Ellen Reece-Jarman

Come Lean on Me
ISBN 978-0-9823390-4-6

HOPE MINISTRIES
Ellen Reece-Jarman
8510 S. Clark Rd
Nashville, MI 49073
hopeministries017@gmail.com

KINGDOM
Ministry
Publications

4801 Willoughby Rd • Holt, MI 48842
☎517-648-6040   📠517-709-3112
kmp@cfcholt.com

TABLE OF CONTENTS

COME LEAN ON ME

Chapter One
SPROUTS AND ICE CREAM

Where HAS the time gone? It is hard for me to believe that on January 1, 2019, I turned 65 years young. 65!! When I was a child, I thought 65 was very old, however now that I am that age, I see it for what it really is . . . just a number.

I remember my grandma telling me age is what you make it. In other words, it's all in the mind. Then I would watch her as she turned to my Grandpa John and in a stern voice say, "For goodness sake, John, act your age."

Grandpa John was so much fun whenever he was around me. He would tease my Grandma Ellen as much as he could get away with. Sometimes he didn't get away with it and ended up going without supper.

My Grandma Ellen stood 4 foot 11 inches tall in her bare feet but, boy oh boy, did she have a temper when she got mad! Not much made her mad as she was an easygoing woman, but for some reason every now and then Grandpa John would do or say something and off the handle she would fly. Her flaming red hair would dance with the wind as she sprang into action and woe betide the person on the receiving end of her anger. On peaceful days her soft green eyes spoke volumes of love especially to my tiny heart. I guess she knew the pain of my world and so did the best she could to bring some happiness to me on the days I stayed at her house with Grandpa John.

Those were happy days for me. I would help Grandpa in his garden picking fresh vegetables for dinner. Until one day I found one vegetable I did NOT like the look of, BRUSSEL SPROUTS; small, round, green little footballs of YUCK! "This is going to be on our plates for dinner tonight," Grandpa John said as he laid the stalk of sprouts into the wheelbarrow.

"Not for me," was my reply. He just looked at me with a warm but concerning smile.

He was right. One sprout was placed on my dinner plate that evening with meat and mashed potatoes. I moved the Brussel Sprout around my plate like it was alive and I held my breath because it smelled horrible. No way was I going to eat that sprout.

Sitting at the dinner table that evening with Grandma and Grandpa I knew I was in trouble. "I want to see a clean plate," Grandma said in a sweet but firm voice. Then the three of us ate in silence.

Looking at the sprout I said to myself, "I do not want this sprout! I do not like Brussel Sprouts!" But the fact remained that it sat staring at me, still sitting on my plate where Grandma had placed it. I sat at the table for a long time. I sat at the table alone. My grandma and grandpa had finished eating and were now sitting in their easy chairs by the glowing fire.

I plucked up the courage and told my grandma that I did not want to eat the sprout. Without looking up she simply said, "Take your plate to the cold cellar, dear." This was a closet by the back kitchen exit door that remained cold. Here food was kept that might otherwise spoil fast, because my grandparents never owned a refrigerator or freezer.

The next morning when I joined my grandparents for breakfast, I asked for something to eat. My grandma told me to go to the cold cellar and bring my plate with the sprout on it back to the table. I did as I was told. The rest of breakfast time I looked at the little green sprout and it looked right back at me. I was hungry so I asked Grandma if I could have a piece of toast. "By all means," she said. "I would love to give you a piece of toast. But first you must eat your sprout."

She was not going to give in and neither was I. I left the table hungry, carrying my dinner plate and sprout back to the cold cellar. This became a routine every mealtime.

Grandpa gave me lots of water to drink, but my tummy hurt from not having any food in it. Then came the time when I made up my mind to eat that ugly green sprout. I carefully carried my plate to the dinner table and just as I was about to pick it up and eat it my grandpa shouted, "STOP!"

At a closer look we saw what appeared to be fur growing from that little green football. It was fur! I ran my finger over the fur. It was very soft! I smiled and then looked up at my grandma who was not smiling at all. Needless to say I was given a good talking to about wasting food. Then one piece of bread and butter was given to me for dinner. Oh it tasted so wonderful! I ate it very slowly savoring every mouthful. From that day on I was never served sprouts again.

I was happy to be named Ellen after my grandma: not because I had flowing red hair or that my hair hung over my right shoulder in one complete ringlet reaching down to my waist or that I had soft green eyes, because I didn't. No. I was proud to be named Ellen after my grandma because she had a kind heart and liked helping people. I spent many happy waking hours by her side in her kitchen watching her work or sitting at her knee helping her roll lengths of yarn into balls ready to be knitted into a sweater.

My grandma was not well educated but she was extremely gifted with her hands. I can still remember two ways in which she supported the family. The first was knitting for other people. One day a lady came to

Grandma's door carrying a photo of a beloved pet that had passed away. The lady gave the picture to my grandma and asked if she would knit that picture into the front of a sweater. Grandma said what she always said, "Come back in three days." After the lady left Grandma started to draw the picture onto white paper counting stitches and colors as she went. She was lost in her thoughts for what seemed like hours.

Grandpa John took me on his knee and helped me understand just what was going on. "Your grandma has to count how many stitches she needs for the ears, the eyes, the nose and so on. Then she has to choose colors and a background that match as close as possible to the picture. Choosing the correct size needles is important too." Once Grandma had everything ready she would study the picture one more time not saying a word to either of us. It wasn't long before I heard the clicking of knitting needles as Grandma set to work on her new project. She stayed focused on the task ahead. Hour after hour click, click, click were the only sounds she made.

It was during Grandma's "busy" time that Grandpa fixed all the meals and each meal was delicious. NO BRUSSEL SPROUTS! He was a good cook and made really interesting and tasteful delights for us to enjoy.

On the third day the lady came back to Grandma's house and Grandma asked her in. Grandpa John had made a nice pot of English tea and as they all sat together happy chatter filled Grandma's parlor. Once the tea things were put away Grandma presented our guest with the finished sweater. Knitted right on the front was the exact picture that was in the photo. A smile of pure joy and delight filled the lady's face as words of deep appreciation mixed with tears of gratitude were expressed. My grandma was paid beyond the asking price and everyone was happy.

Another time I was staying with them a gentleman called. So Grandpa John invited him in. The man had ballroom gowns that needed a sequined design sown on each of them. The sequins had to be sown on one at a time by hand which would not have been a problem except there were sixteen dresses. Grandma and the man talked over the design and Grandpa John and I sat listening. A price was agreed on and Grandma told the man to come back in three days.

Grandpa hung a metal bar across the corner of the parlor on which all sixteen dresses were hung. Grandma stood for hours sewing the sequin pattern onto each dress. Over the next three days she was buried in those beautiful dresses. Each dress had many layers of tulle, but only the top layer needed the sequin pattern on it. I held the box of sequins for Grandma as she painstakingly sowed each one on by hand following the design she had been given.

Sure enough, on the third day the man returned and examined Grandma's work with a fine-toothed comb. "Excellent," he kept saying, "excellent!" Once all the dresses were loaded into his car and he drove away, Grandma turned to us with her cute Irish smile and said, "Put on your hats and coats. It's ice cream time!" Ice cream was a real treat not experienced very often, but oh boy was today ever different. We walked the short distance to the ice cream parlor, ordered cones and sat around a small decorative table licking our vanilla ice cream very slowly until it was all gone.

This was the way that my grandma supported her family. She was never out of work. She was such a gifted grandma.

Grandpa John, on the other hand, liked to work in the garden growing all types of vegetables, some to sell to the ma and pa stores nearby and some for market. He was a strong man for his five foot frame carrying large amounts of freshly dug potatoes and other vegetables in brown burlap sacks over his shoulders to place in the wheelbarrow that waited at the end of the garden plot. He would hum as he worked the vegetable patch day after day. Grandpa John said it was very important to grow healthy vegetables for young families to enjoy.

On market day he would load up his wheelbarrow full to the brim with all kinds of colorful vegetables and together we would set off to the market place while it was still dark. I would hold on to the hem of his jacket, as he needed both hands on the wheelbarrow. We would sing or hum during the mile long walk to town while most people were still sleeping. The market place soon came alive with activity as vendors got in place to sell their goods. And happy chatter turned into DEAL OF THE DAY!

Grandpa John turned to me and said, "The early bird catches the worm." I thought to myself, "Who wants worms?" He read my facial expression and smiled down at me explaining the meaning behind the remark. "Bargains are found by the early risers," he said. "I guess that makes sense," was my reply.

Our wheelbarrow was empty within two hours of being at market. Grandpa John cleaned the wheelbarrow, picked me up, sat me gently on the folded liner and pushed me all the way home. Leaning over to help me out he whispered, "Little One, lean on me." As we walked in the door, Grandma had oatmeal and toast ready for us to enjoy. Happy days. Happy memories.

COME LEAN ON ME

Chapter
Two
A
PERFECT
FIT

The mind is a wonderful thing. It has the capacity to store up so much information for our pleasure or for our pain. Either way this information is available to us twenty-four/seven. My mind likes to travel back to happy memories and recall the times of my youth. One such memory is when I met for the first time the man I knew would one day be my husband. David was 25 and I was 16 when we met in 1969. It was love at first sight for both of us. After several months of dating, we decided to go wedding shopping in Exeter, Devon, England. The main high street was very long and filled with all kinds of shops selling wedding outfits for all types of budgets. David went one way and I went the other. We planned on meeting up for lunch to compare our bargains.

I had never taken my clothes off so many times in one day. By lunchtime I had not found anything that was within the budget. Feeling somewhat discouraged, I met David for lunch. He had the biggest, most handsome smile on his face. A brief kiss told me he had found his outfit. How come most guys can find their outfit within a very short time of looking, and we girls look much harder and longer to find just the right outfit for our special day?

Over lunch he said he would come with me the rest of the day and help me find my dress and accessories. He was true to his word. For most of the afternoon we entered and exited many shops but found nothing we both liked. As the day started to draw to a close and I was no further forward in finding my outfit, he too was getting discouraged. At the last shop available to look in, David said he would wait outside so in I went, alone. Two older ladies greeted me with a warm smile and asked how they might help. I was close to tears as I shared my story of the day. Both ladies listened with kindness written all over their sweet little faces and then said, "We believe we may have the dress you have been looking for." They led me to a bridal changing room at the back of the shop. Once again I removed my clothes and they helped fit me into a dress.

A PERFECT FIT! I stood in front of the mirror not daring to believe this dress would be within my budget. Both ladies fussed over me like I was their long lost daughter then stood back to admire their work. "Perfect fit in every way, my dear," said one of them to me. "May we tell you the story behind this dress?" the other said.

"Yes, please," I said as I stood looking at this beautiful wedding dress hugging my tiny frame.

"You see this is a hand made to order dress. A doctor had it specially made for his daughter, but alas, she decided not to go through with her wedding so the doctor donated her dress to the store and told us to give it away to bless another." That meant IT WAS FREE TO ME! My heart took flight knowing that this dress was well within our budget.

After getting dressed we called David into the store and told him the story. He smiled and hugged both ladies. He also made a financial donation to help another. My full-length white silk dress was covered with a white lace full-length coat. The trim was soft white down that gently moved in the breeze, perfect for an October wedding. David's pin striped black suit was also a perfect fit. We were a perfect couple. David and I were married October 31, 1969 on a dry but very windy day. The Church of England parish was high on a harbor key side overlooking the harbor where little boats were bobbing up and down in the current. It was the perfect view.

*God is our refuge
and strength,
a very present help
in trouble.*

—Psalm 46:1 (KJV).

Chapter Three
**A BUNDLE OF
JOY**

After three years as man and wife Cordelia Jayne was born, a perfect daughter in every way. Within a few months it was discovered I was with child again. Excited yet somewhat overwhelmed we prepared for baby number two.

Devlin Stacey was born November 5, 1974, Guy Fawkes Night. As fireworks filled the night sky, I smiled and thought, "All of England is celebrating the birth of my son." Cordelia had a little brother and we had a son. Now our little family was complete.

Dee was a wonderful big sister. I would watch her as she gently stroked Devlin's head while I was nursing him. Dee would sing lullabies that came from her tiny heart as a gift of her love for her little brother. It was Dee's job to place his socks on his feet, which made me smile because she got the big toe outside the sock each time. Still Dee was determined and with lots of practice, mastered the job very well for a child not yet two.

Many happy days followed Devlin's birth. Dee and I would bathe our babies together. We each had a baby bath with baby cream and lotions at the ready. Dee would watch what I did with Devlin and she would do the same with her baby doll, singing as we went. David would watch us from his easy chair and smile with pride.

Christmas was fast approaching and this year another stocking was added to the other three. I had hand made these and had written our names on each one: Daddy, Mummy, Dee and Devlin. We placed the stockings on either side of the fireplace to complete our Christmas decorations. The week leading up to Christmas my family would sit all together on the couch. David would hold the children while I got a soft blanket to cover us all. Then David would tell us a story before Dee went to bed. This precious family time was filled with love and tender moments of togetherness.

Stepping into 1975 I wondered what the year would hold for my family and myself. I was soon to find the answer. An answer I never expected. An answer I never wanted. An answer that would change my life and my family forever.

My mother had moved into the area and wanted to see her first grandson. We arranged to meet for one o'clock lunch at the local coffee shop in town. On the given day I nursed my son and put him down for his mid-morning nap. I got busy cleaning the house just in case she came back for a visit. I found the cutest outfit for Dee and laid it on my bed next to the white wool outfit that David had bought for Devlin while I was still pregnant with him. I chose long black pants and a thick royal blue sweater for myself. Everything was ready. Now to wake up my son, change his diaper, nurse him one more time and put him into his darling little outfit. My plan was to dress the children warmly, place them in the pram under a warm blanket and push them to town. Only this day, that would all change.

As I entered his room I said, "Wake up little man, you are going to meet your grandmother." I opened his curtains and turned to look at him. He was still. I moved closer and reached down and picked him up turning him to face me. Then I saw. Then I knew. Then my heart split in two and my mouth went dry. I placed my tiny son back into his crib and went to dial the emergency services. It wasn't long before I heard the siren.

Unceremoniously scooping Dee into my arms I ran across the street to my neighbor's house. I pounded on the door and screamed Sylvia's name. Once the door was opened I quickly deposited Dee into unsuspecting arms. I told Sylvia to call David and tell him to meet me at the hospital. Running back across the street I met the ambulance at my door and led a tiny white haired man in uniform up the stairs to Devlin's room. He gently wrapped my son in his baby blanket and took him to the waiting ambulance with me in hot pursuit.

During the ride to the hospital the white haired ambulance attendant held my baby lovingly. I looked at him and he looked at me with tears in his compassionate blue eyes. I asked pleadingly if my baby was going to be all right. Looking at Devlin he softly answered, "He is in the arms of Jesus now." I sat there empty and numb not knowing what to do or say. I did not understand. I never knew all hope of saving my son was long gone. I never knew I would never nurse my baby at my breast again. I never knew.

It wasn't long before we were at the hospital where he had been born just eight weeks before. This time we were in a small, sad, sterile emergency room instead of the happy maternity wing. The kind old ambulance man placed the tiny, still body of my son on an enormous bed and left the room. I heard a noise and turned to see a doctor walking through the doorway. He looked right at me as he approached the bed.

This brand new, young emergency room doctor opened the baby blanket, took one look at my tiny son and in a professional tone said to me, "Your son is dead." He did not look at me as he said this. His words cut through me like a hot knife through butter. I screamed, grabbed the sleeves of his bright white coat and pushed him toward my baby. I pleaded with him, screamed at him to help my son. But he could not help him. He was not God.

My anger exploded, a monster I could not control. The doctor tried to protect himself against my constant blows, but one of my flailing fists caught him on the side of his face and sent him flying into the hand washbasin. He hit his head hard enough to knock himself out. I screeched for someone else to come help my baby.

My out of control emotions only brought a very large, very round female nurse running through the door with a gift for me: a very large, very scary looking needle which she plunged into my arm. I don't remember any more until I woke up next to David sitting beside my bed in a darkened room. His beautiful brown eyes were swollen and red from all the tears he had shed.

As we looked at each other, guilt took hold of me and I heard myself sobbing to him, "I'm so very sorry, I failed you in taking good care of your son." David could not speak. He reached over and placed a gentle kiss on my forehead and we cried together.

When we were emotionally ready we walked home from the hospital, a very different walk from any other we had taken. There were no newborn babies in

David's arms. No happy smiles. No warm greetings from friends and neighbors; only a cloud of sadness and grief. We were so wrapped up in the deepest pain ever felt by a parent, that of the loss of their child, that we saw no one around us. We were totally alone.

My head spun with the horror of the day. I struggled with unimaginable guilt, overwhelming sadness and all-encompassing grief. Unanswerable questions frantically spun through my head. I leaned on David, clutching his arm. But I did not really notice that he was there.

As we got closer to our house I felt myself pulling back, slowing down. I did not want to go in there again. I did not want to see the clothes on the bed or the baby bath that I had gotten ready to bathe him in. I did not want to face it all again. It was too much. David gently led me on.

Dee's voice broke through the roar in my head. Smiling and chattering she ran to greet us and give us hugs. David picked her up and nuzzled her neck. She laughed. She was good medicine. The fog lifted, a little. The questions slowed, but did not stop. The pain was too deep.

The following days until Devlin's cremation passed in a fog. I could still hear him crying and see him around the house. My breasts ached to feed him, my arms to hold him. Precious memories and painful memories all mixed into one. The questions constantly throbbed in my head. I was intensely preoccupied with thoughts and images of Devlin's death. My mind would not let go of the pain. I started to shatter.

If only I knew then what I know now: that the Man of sorrow, so acquainted with death, could bring the greatest comfort of all to this broken heart. If only I had known of Jesus. How different things would have been. I could have embraced Him and not the depression setting in. I could have allowed the Son of God to embrace me and carry me on His wings of hope to a place of quiet and rest from the turmoil of my soul. If only I had known He was waiting, just waiting, with outstretched arms and an invitation to be part of my life, but I did not know. No one told me about Jesus.

As I waited to say my farewells to my son at the crematorium my world grew blacker. David and I stood at the reception door waiting for the hearse to arrive. No hearse came. Instead a regular four-door black sedan pulled up. The driver, dressed all in black, got out of the car and opened the trunk. He reached in and gently lifted out a small brown cardboard box and took it into the chapel. As David and I entered the chapel, we saw him place the tiny box on a conveyer belt ready to be sent behind the white curtains. Rage filled my soul. No coffin? Nothing to say he was special? Wasn't my baby worth more than that?

The chapel was filled with close friends and family sitting motionless in mourning.

Only a single red rose on the cardboard box spoke to me of hope that day. After a moment of silence, the music started and the conveyer belt moved the box slowly through open stark white curtains that slowly closed behind it. The music continued to play as every one filed silently out of the chapel. That was it. The end of a life. No talking, no luncheon, no hugs . . . nothing. David and I got in our rental car and drove away. Empty. The blackness was descending. I shattered more.

If I knew then what I know now my head and heart would have been lifted in total appreciation for the bundle of joy now resting in the arms of Jesus and not mine. He could have changed my emotional state. He could have stopped me from shattering.

As it was, I found myself in a corner curled up in a fetal position, tossing and turning, hearing nothing other than the cries of Devlin. In my mind I cried, screamed in torment. "Make it stop! Make the pain stop! Someone save me! Someone help me!"

But no one could hear me. I was not speaking out loud. I was so numb with pain that the outside world did not exist to me. I felt no one come to help me. I felt nothing. No hope. I was spiraling downward into darkness. Not even a flicker of light. I was numb. I saw no lifeline.

Then I heard something that snapped me back to reality. Something inside of me snapped like a twig across the knee. Our family doctor and my husband were talking by my side. Dr. Peter Monahan said I was no good, beyond help and that David should place me in a sanatorium and take another wife. Then the doctor said David should be intimate with another woman. I was jerked out of the all-encompassing empty darkness that was swallowing me. I let him have it verbally. No one but me was going to be intimate with my husband.

Apparently these were the only words I had spoken in months. Someone, something had finally reached me. Someone had opened my ears. Someone had finally heard my cries. It could only have been God. He is the only one who could have reached so deep into my soul. He is the only one who could have rescued me from this bottomless pit of nothingness and despair.

In our 7 years of marriage David and I never talked about Jesus. We never went to church or opened a Bible. Not that we were against it we just never knew. So over the months following Devlin's death we sunk into a pit of despair over the loss of an innocent child.

Now I know there is only one person who can ever meet the deepest pain of a child lost and that is the person of Jesus Christ. We did not thrive as parents. We survived as parents. How different that would have been if the Spirit of God had been an active part of our lives. We were in a world of darkness that needed the light of Jesus Christ, but we never gave Him a consideration. How different things would have been if we had. Jesus is the great physician, the mighty comforter, the healer of our souls. We missed out.

After the incident with David and Dr. Monahan, life started looking up. But I still fought with very harsh negative emotions. I would take Dee for walks and see new mothers pushing their newborn babies and ask if I could look in their prams. Then I would find myself happy for them and extremely jealous at the same time. I felt the injustice and unfairness of losing Devlin. I had no support group. No connection to other grieving parents. No professional counseling or services of any kind to help me through. I did what I could with the constant help of David, but it was a slow difficult uphill climb.

Devlin Stacey
born on November fifth 1974
died eight weeks later on January fifth 1975.
SIDS took the life of my beautiful tiny first-born son

COME LEAN ON ME

Chapter Four
TRIGGER HAPPY

It is said that time is the great healer and so it was for us. As time passed I found out we were expecting again. Still in a state of healing, we slowly managed to prepare for the new addition to our family. About this time my husband David, who was in the Territorial Army part time, told me of a "Shoot Off" weekend that had been planned for all the soldiers and their wives to compete in. "Put my name down, please," I said. He took one look at my growing belly and said, "No way!" Needless to say I worked on changing his mind and we became part of the Tiverton team.

Lying on the ground to shoot the self-loading rifle was a bit of a challenge as I was so pregnant, however that's what sand bags are for, right? Before long I was able to lie on the ground of the quarry with my tummy safely inside the sandbag and shoot at the target that I could not really see. I did hit it but my score was low. Oh well, the hand pistol competition after lunch would bring up my team's score, I hoped.

Throughout lunch David kept reminding me to lock my elbows when I pull the trigger because of the recoil. I was listening, honest I was! My name was called and David gave me his Magnum 44 hand pistol to hold. It was heavy and I was nervous, but feeling very confident with David standing behind me, I squeezed the trigger and BANG! With my turn finished, I handed off the gun to my husband. "Let's walk to the top of the quarry," he said. Once inside the waiting ambulance I was handed a small round mirror and told to look at my face. I had not listened to David's warning about keeping my elbows locked when I pulled the trigger of the Magnum 44 hand pistol. The recoil brought the end of the barrel back towards my face. I saw that the end on the barrel had hit my face and opened up the skin. "I'm dead!" were the first words out of my mouth and David and the ambulance driver burst into laughter. Yuck! I hated the taste of blood!

A little to the right and I would have lost my eye. As it was all I got was my face washed, a patch over my eye and a pat on the back for being so brave. At my check up with my family doctor, Dr. Peter Monahan told me I was very fortunate not to have lost my right eye.

A few months later I gave birth to our second son, Richard Leon, perfect in every way. This time I would not fail as a mother. I would not fail as a wife. This time this son would grow up to enjoy the fullness of life. And so it was, our little family was once again complete.

I wrote this poem to my husband David to remind him just how much I loved him, and to tell him that he was my everything.

POEM FOR DAVID
by Ellen

From the beginning of time Love says, "You are mine"
Gathering the sands from every shore.
The love we share meant so much more...
From every blade of fresh green grass,
Our love will bloom, Our love will last.

We have a gift beyond compare,
Surpassing all, because we care,
This test of time, has made us see
That I belong to you, and you belong to me.

Touching of souls, united from above
Resting secure in the warm arms of love.
A hug goodnight, tenderly holding you tight,
I smooth your hair, to show I care,

A kiss to embrace your beautiful face
As we snuggle down together.
What could be better? Who could ask for more,
Then for this love to continue, for this love to soar
Free on the wings of the purest white dove
With the powerful potion, we call....LOVE!!

One day David and I received an invitation to a wedding from a longtime friend of his. I was hesitant to go without my infant son, but David reassured me that our son would be well cared for. When the wedding day arrived, I dressed Dee in a new outfit and shoes we had bought for this special event. The white lace dress and baby blue jacket that hugged her tiny body perfectly, white lace socks and white shoes completed her fairy tale princess outfit. She was the first one ready. I gave her a few toys and books and told her to play on the rug in the family room while I went to get ready. She looked up at me with a smile that could melt the snows of Alaska and said, " Dee-Dee good girl." I gave her a gentle kiss on her sweet little head and off I went.

When I returned to the family room, David was sitting ready and waiting in his easy chair, but where was Dee?

I stood there for a moment in sheer fear, then asked him in an elevated voice where Dee was. "I thought she was with you," came his reply.

"NO! She is NOT with me!" We stood in silence each looking at one another wondering where our precious child could have gone, when we heard a faint sound coming from the open fireplace chimney. David moved closer. We listened again, nothing.

David said, "Dee-Dee, where are you hiding?" in a voice that he would often use the times he played hide and seek with his daughter. Dee-Dee said, "Up here

Daddy! Me stuck!" David quickly stripped down to his undies and went up the chimney after his daughter. Sure enough she was stuck in place. Reassuring her that this was a game, he made sure to protect her face and arms as he gently but firmly tugged at her ankles. Sure enough she came down in a large puff of very black soot. He too was covered. I burst out laughing seeing the two of them sitting in the fireplace hugging on each other as black as black could be. I cleaned Dee up and soon had her ready to go this time in the only clean clothes she had, her pajamas. Off David, Dee and I went to the wedding. After the wedding, we shared the story that had many guests rolling in their seats with laughter. Oh happy days!

Our family lived in government housing and out of compassion shortly after Devlin had died we were moved from one government house to another so that we could all continue to heal from the sad memories of the death of Devlin. It was in this house that I began receiving obscene phone calls that had me in a state of fear for my life and the lives of my family. We asked the government to move us again for safety reasons, but they said no and told us to contact the police. We did and a phone tap was put in place. Over the next few weeks the calls continued with no sign of catching the culprit. David was due to leave for his mandatory weekend Territorial Army training. I begged him not to go. Sensing my fear, he put a plan of action in place to keep the children and me safe. There were eleven steps leading from the front entrance hallway to our bedrooms upstairs. David counted up seven steps and loosened the carpet rod that held the carpet in place. Next he put in place what is now called bubble wrap and gave me clear instruction for my next step. That night like always I "read" a made up story to our two children, sang them a song, kissed them both goodnight and prepared myself for bed. I was just drifting off to sleep when I heard my front door open and close. Fear gripped me. I could hear my heart beating inside my ears. My body felt paralyzed, but I knew I had to move.

I heard someone moving around downstairs inside my house. This was it. Now to put David's plan into action. I carefully reached down under my side of the bed to where David had placed his Magnum 44 hand pistol and wrapped my hand around the cold iron handle. I quietly crept out of bed and positioned myself against the closed in balcony. With my two hands holding the gun and my two knees knocking against each other I waited, trying my best to control my breathing.

The intruder was now mounting the stairs. One, two, three, all I kept thinking about was how to keep David's children safe. Four, five, six, this was it. One more step and I would commit murder. I held my breath waiting for step seven to be taken. Waiting for the bubble wrap to make its noise as it popped.

"FREEZE SUCKER!" I shouted as fear sprung my body into action. There I stood at the top of the stairway, legs spread wide, elbows locked in place and the Magnum 44 inches away from the face of my intruder. My right index finger found the trigger and as I squeezed it, I waited for the loudest bang ever to sound out into the cold, quite night.

"DON'T SHOOT! DON'T SHOOT!" said my intruder, his face turning a whiter shade of pale. The man standing within inches of the end of the barrel was my own husband David. Once our minds and hearts adjusted to this near death experience, I was full of questions. Why had he not gone with his unit? Why did he come back home in the middle of the night? Why did he not phone me to say he was coming home early? Questions, questions.

David and I went into the kitchen where he made a lovely pot of tea. He explained that he had missed his connection because of a flat tire he had to deal with. He didn't phone me to say he was coming home in case I thought it was the bad guy. Why didn't your gun fire? I asked him. He smiled and showed me that I had forgotten to lift off the safety clip on the side. I burst into tears and he held me and laughed. "Come; lean on me," he said as he took my hand. We went to bed thankful that sometimes I didn't listen well to what he told me. We went to bed smiling. We went to bed as man and wife.

The police eventually caught the man whose obscene phone calls had filled my heart with fear. We did move again; this time to another part of Tiverton. It was in this new house where happy times were once again filling our lives. Our daughter Dee was going to have a birthday. David and I planned a great celebration inviting thirty plus friends and their children to share this special day. After all, turning four was very important!!

Party streamers were in place. Balloons were everywhere. There was lots and lots of food for the 30 guests plus children. Party games were going on inside and outside the house. All I had left to do was put the candles on Dee's birthday cake when I heard a very loud crash coming from the family room. I walked in to find David on the floor. He was very still.

As I knelt down beside him to listen for a heartbeat I knew would not be there, my chest became tight with fear. This was a repeat of what I experienced with our son Devlin. I tried to tell myself everything would be all right. I tried to believe that David had passed out from all the day's excitement. I kept telling myself, over and over again in my mind, "not again, please not again."

After hearing no heart beat for what seemed like forever, I sprang into action and called the emergency service a second time. I heard the siren a second time. I saw the emergency personnel come in and take David's body away. I didn't see my guests leave. I didn't see who cleaned up everything. David was gone. Devlin was gone. I was still here. Now who will I lean on? Now who will take care of our children and me? Seven wonderful years of marriage to a wonderful, caring, gentle man. My soul mate, my everything was gone forever. Now what?

David died from a heart attack that no one saw coming. He died at his daughter's fourth birthday surrounded by those that loved him.

He will forever be missed.

Trust in the Lord with all your heart, and lean not on your own understanding; in all your ways acknowledge him, and he shall direct your paths.

—Proverbs 3:5-6 (KJV).

Chapter Five
THE OTHER ME

I am not proud of the days, weeks, and months that followed David's death. I was so very angry. I wanted to hurt someone like I was hurting. One day a local minister came calling to my house and tried to bring some words of comfort to my shattered heart. I listened out of politeness wishing in my heart that he would just shut up and go away. I was so angry with God for taking so much from me in my young life that the minister's so-called words of comfort and compassion fell on deaf ears. Before he left I asked him "What makes God hurt the most?"

"Sin," he replied.

I asked, "What is sin?"

He listed many things, among them taking another woman's husband. He made it very clear that in the Holy Scriptures it says to keep the marriage bed holy. In other words do not steal someone else's husband to meet your own desires. Sex was the last thing on my mind. But the thought of feeling a man's strong arms of protection around me and his passionate embrace made me miss David even more. Knowing I was still young and attractive, I figured I could use this to my advantage. I could have a man's arms, hurt God and keep my family all at the same time. My thoughts were only about getting even with God for the pain I believed God caused me. I had lost enough. I would not let Him take any more from me.

Over the next months I did all I could to hurt God. I did not realize the only person I was hurting was myself. Depression and thoughts of suicide were my constant companions. Migraines took much of my energy. The medicine from the doctor would knock me out for hours at a time, but did nothing to take away the horrible headaches.

I doted on my children. They were my world. Yet I felt inadequate to give them the love they deserved. Money was not an object as I had a widow's allowance from the government. We lacked for nothing. Still I missed David. My heart ached constantly. My brother's girlfriend, Carole, came to live with us. She shared chores and helped me with the children. She was a tower of strength during the times I was unable to cope. She never complained. She was so easy-going and happy all the time. Even though she worked a full time job she still had time to help take care of us. We spent time laughing and doing things together. One evening after the children were in bed we decided to watch a movie. I made bacon sandwiches and hot chocolate and we sat down to watch a horror movie. Big Mistake. After we were good and scared it was time to go to bed. As we climbed the stairs, the lid to the letter slot in our front door banged three times. We jumped and grabbed each other. We ran into the kitchen where I grabbed a knife and then called the cops. Still shaking and holding on to each other when the policeman arrived we talked over each other trying to explain that we were two women alone with small children and someone had been banging the lid to the mail slot and running away. He sat with us on the stairs facing the front door. Here we would be able to see an outline of anyone banging on the letterbox through the frosted glass in the door. A few minutes passed and the letterbox banged again. He turned and asked with a smile if that was what we heard. "That's it!" I yelled. "Grab him!" "How can I grab the wind?" he teased. With a glint in his eye, a tilt of his hat and a tease in his voice he said, "Good night, ladies. Sleep well." All tension gone, Carole and I laughed so hard we had to lean on each other to make it up the stairs to our separate bedrooms.

Carole helped fill the void, a little, but my heart still ached. Nothing completely filled the void. No matter how much "fun" I had I still felt empty. No matter how many bars I visited or dance halls I frequented I still felt alone. Nothing could bring back Devlin or David. And to add to my sadness Carole got married and moved away.

The pit of despair became deeper and darker. The monster living inside me was unrelenting. It kept filling my head with lies; lies that I was worthless, that everything I valued would die, that nothing I did was worth the effort. And some days it did take effort. Lots of effort. More effort than I wanted to give sometimes. The feelings of loneliness were getting worse instead of better. The world seemed darker, not brighter. Would this pain never end? Was I losing interest in life? I could not lift myself from the miry clay. I was stuck. My desire to hurt God did not seem to be working. Or at least it did not give me any satisfaction. I only felt more and more empty. More and more lonely. More and more desperate.

The monster in my head kept telling me that my children would be better off with another family, one with a mother and a father to love and care for them. That this pain and emptiness would never go away unless I made it. And I could do just that. The medicine cabinet held a permanent solution to a temporary problem. I gathered together all the pills and potions calling to me from the medicine cabinet and placed them together in a cereal bowl on the kitchen table.

A knock came on my front door. Not now, I thought. But the knock was insistent. I answered it. There stood God's introduction to a new life. God had a plan in place for my life and it was starting to unfold. God used this beautiful Christian brother called Graham to lead me into the everlasting open arms of Christ. After receiving Christ as my personal Savior I started attending church at King Street Gospel Hall, Tiverton, Devon, a Brethren fellowship that taught the fullness and truth of the word of God. It was a time to begin.

COME LEAN ON ME

Chapter Six
TIME TO GROW

Learning to read for the first time at age 23 was a challenge at best; however, I learned that prayer changes things and within the first year I had graduated to self-taught lessons. Hillary had been an excellent teacher that first year, so loving, patient and kind, but now I was ready to claim the victory in Jesus' name and for his glory. I was ready to step up and step out in faith and let Jesus be my teacher.

Over the next few months I went to every service King Street offered: twice on Sunday, midweek prayer meetings, and home Bible studies. I was growing deeper and deeper in love with the Savior of my soul. Weekends my children and I would often stay with Graham and his lovely wife, Heather. They became my spiritual parents and together mentored my children and me in the values God intended us to live by. It was during an evening service at church that God spoke clearly into my heart. "Look over there," He said. "That man is going to be your new husband." Talk about shocked! At the end of the service and while standing at the back of the church, Heather told me to introduce myself to the "man over there." I tried to argue the point, but Heather was determined, so over we went. Alan was standing with Johnathan, the youth pastor who had lead him to the Lord some months earlier. I tried to engage Alan in conversation, but his smart mouth answers set my blood to boiling. We did NOT hit it off and I was glad when Heather said it was time to go.

I have heard it said that God works in mysterious ways, and so it was with this new encounter with Alan. He called my house some time later to ask if he could visit and meet my two children. I said only if he came with the youth pastor. Alan and Johnathan came calling that next Friday night bearing gifts. Alan brought a big red plastic fire truck for Richard and a beautiful large doll for Dee. I was taken aback. Then he took off his coat and lay on my floor with the children while Johnathan and I looked on. It made my heart so happy to see my children giggle with delight at their new toys. It looked so natural. It felt so right. Was it in God's plan? As the two men got ready to leave for the evening, Johnathan invited us to tea at his house the following Sunday. Before I could reply, both my children said, "YES, PLEASE!" so the invitation was accepted.

At Johnathan's house, after tea was over and we were about to leave, Alan grabbed me and kissed me. I slapped him and he smiled and asked me to be his wife. God's plan was unfolding in my life. The following weekend Alan took me to meet his parents. Ralph and Dulcie were very hospitable and we got on really well together. The next morning after breakfast Alan told his parents that he was going to marry me. Out of concern, his parents shared their thoughts about his taking on a ready-made family and asked him if he really understood that this was a package deal. Alan stood and made it very clear that he did.

Over the months leading up to our wedding in September, Dulcie and Ralph would visit one weekend a month getting to know the children and me. I had never known this kind of mother. She was very understanding, kind, gentle and patient with me and the children. I found myself opening up to her and trusting her to mentor me in family values and how to be a mother.

God gave me a new husband and the children a new father. "Lean on me," Alan said, "for I will always take care of you and the children." We were married at King Street Gospel Hall, Tiverton, Devon, England on September 1, 1979. That was where we first met. That was where we were baptized, so it felt only right that we should be married there. Mr. Fred Britton officiated and Mr. Ven Webber was registrar. Ninety guests prayed with us and wished us God's richest blessings in the coming years. Our life as man and wife was just beginning, but I felt in my heart it would be an adventure of a lifetime.

During the years that followed there were many changes. A year after we were married our daughter Rebecca was born. A short time after, God made it possible to buy a house. We were pleased as this would be a good place to bring up our children. We moved into town and soon our fourth child, Matthew, was born.

Dee, our oldest daughter, became an instant mother to her younger brother. Although there was ten years difference in age, Dee took to caring for her baby brother like a duck takes to water. Apart from nursing him, Dee was there to care for many of his needs. I would watch her sit by his crib and hold his little hand as she sang him to sleep. Then she would lie down as close as possible and read her book. During his early years, Dee would often carry Matthew on her hip or sit him in her lap while she read a story to all her siblings. Richard and Rebecca would play together in the fenced in large back garden, while Dee would be sitting on a blanket with her little brother enjoying being close.

As time passed, Alan decided to establish his own business selling tools. He was a self-motivator and gone long hours, but every Sunday he spent attending church and catching up on family time. One weekend a month Mom and Dad Jarman would come and stay with us. I watched as the bond of love and family grew stronger. I had never felt so secure, cared for and loved.

Alan felt a call to go to Bible school. He shared this desire with the church leadership and one of our elders encouraged Alan to apply to Gospel Literature Outreach (GLO) in Scotland. Alan applied and was accepted for their one-year training course. He left for school leaving me home with four little ones under ten. I did not want to be alone again. I leaned on God to bring me someone to stay with me during the time that Alan was gone. A young woman in our church was looking for accommodations and God made a way for her to move in with us. The more I leaned on God for support the more I saw answers to prayers.

Alan came home from GLO full of a desire to serve God full time. The home we had in the center of Tiverton became a place of fellowship, prayer and spiritual guidance at lunch times for the youth of our church and community. Alan and I would seek the Lord during our morning devotions for godly wisdom in dealing with our onslaught of visitors. When counseling or giving advice we wanted to give only godly advice. We believed it was not our opinion that mattered it was what God said that counted.

Be strong and courageous. Do not be afraid or terrified because of them, for the LORD your God goes with you; He will never leave you nor forsake you.

— Deuteronomy 31:6 (NIV).

Chapter Seven
ADVENTURES ON
THE MISSION FIELD

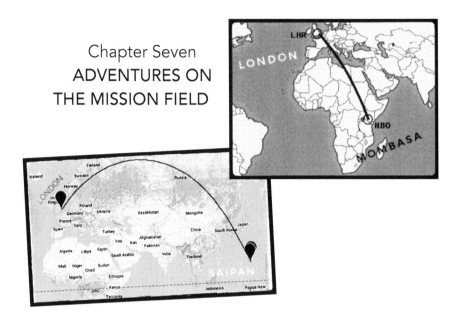

In 1985 Alan felt the Lord call him to go to Kenya, East Africa. He shared this with our church leadership for their prayers and spiritual guidance. They gave their blessing and Alan traveled to London to join a YWAM (Youth With a Mission) team headed for Mombasa for a summer of service. When he returned from his four-month adventure in Kenya, he was filled with stories of the many miracles God had done during his time there. The Mombasa sand had gotten under his toes. We sold our house, packed up our four young children, packed four suitcases and in 1986 we left England for the adventure of a lifetime.

Arriving in Mombasa, Kenya, East Africa we found out just how much of an adventure it was going to be. Youth With A Mission (YWAM) had a very small, one-bedroom house ready for us, a family of 6, to live in. Culture-shocked and jet-lagged we found ourselves having to ask for help with everyday needs. One of these needs - water. The small house had a faucet over a white square enamel sink in the kitchen, but once we turned it open, no water came out. The small house had a toilet and shower room, but no water.

We soon learned how to make a water catchment inside our home for personal use. Water pipes ran under ground from Mombasa town to the Indian Ocean. In the early morning the water ran to fill up the hotels in and around Mombasa tourist area. The remaining water trickled down towards the ocean through pipes connected with our mission base location.

Our next door neighbor had eight children so he would get up at 3 A.M. to open fully his water taps allowing any water running to fill his catchments for that day's use. We too needed to catch water, so I got up at 2 A.M. and opened our taps to fill our water containers. The two families had to share whatever water came down the pipes sometimes only catching half the amount each family needed for that day.

Alan and I had joined YWAM to become Bible students. The Discipleship Training School lasted six months and at the end of that time we were invited to become full time voluntary staff. Alan joined Mercy Ministry and worked along side brother Jared Okoth. God placed me in the preschool working along side Rose Kivunike. Two wonderful years and many adventures later God called us back to cold wet England for a time of rest.

In 1989 God opened up the way for us to return to the mission field. We received a welcome invitation to join the staff of Youth With A Mission, Saipan. God confirmed this calling through the Holy Scriptures: Proverbs 25:25, "Like cold water to a weary soul is good news from a distant land." Saipan was to be our new home.

This time Dee, our oldest, wanted to remain in England for her school and college education. This was going to be the first time that one of our children would be separated from us. Emotions ran high in every family member. After much prayer and talking feelings through, Dee stayed in England with close friends Roy and Maureen. Dee was happy to be part of their family.

Richard, Rebecca, Matthew, Alan and I went to Saipan; a distance of 7,244 miles away from Dee for the next ten years of service. For the first three years we were on staff with YWAM. Richard, Rebecca and Matthew attended Grace Christian Academy School on the island.

Located in the Northern Marianas Island, this tropical island gave us many happy hours of ministry and quality family time. During our time on Saipan we met a couple from Michigan - James and Naomi. They had four children like us. Over the three years they were on the island, our two families spent much time together. Alan and James would often go diving. The Pacific Ocean was warm and held many interesting things to see. The Grotto was one such place. It was a stunning, collapsed cave and was excellent for snorkeling and scuba diving although swimming was not allowed due to the current of the incoming and outgoing tide. After descending the one hundred and fifty very slippery steps, the guys would buddy up and with tanks, weights, and fins enter the warm Pacific Ocean to enjoy the many tropical species of fish and coral.

Our friendship deepened over time and when it came time for James and Naomi to return to the USA many tears were shed. God had a plan in place only we never knew it at that time.

Alan and I remained on the island of Saipan seven more years and established our own ministry called Stepping Stones Ministries, separate from YWAM. We believed that this name portrayed stepping from darkness into the light. God's Holy Word came alive through outreach and ministering in the prison, as well as teaching it in our school. Alan worked in prison ministry, and I taught two back-to-back classes Kindergarten and First grade in our home for the island children. God abundantly blessed and prospered both ministries way beyond our expectations.

In 2000 our path was once again redirected back to England. This was a good time to reconnect with family and friends. It was also a good time to visit with the many churches and individuals that supported our family and ministry. We began seeking the Lord for the next step.

For with God nothing shall be impossible.

— Luke 1:37 (KJV)

COME LEAN ON ME

Chapter Eight
OUR NEW
HOME

In 2001 God made a way for us to leave England once again. This time it was not a tropical island. This time there was no warm ocean to swim in. This time it was our youngest daughter Rebecca that wanted to stay in England and complete her school and college education. Emotions ran high inside of me. My mind was full of questions. I had to lean on God. I had to trust by faith that this next move was part of His plan. So Alan, Matthew and I left cold, wet England for Michigan, USA.

Richard was not with us as he had married a wonderful lady named Amy while we were living on Saipan and they had moved to the USA to live.

Naomi was waiting at the airport to greet us and bring us to our first American home. James and Naomi gave us their full live-in basement as our new home while Alan worked and we saved to buy our own home. Over the months we looked at many houses, but never felt they were where God would have us live so we decided to do what Gideon did and put out a fleece before God. Judges 6 tells us that Gideon put out a fleece for God to give him direction. We asked God to give us a sign that we would know which house was to be our new home.

This is the fleece we told only God. The owner of the house would sell their family pet with the house. A few days later we went to see another house. This three bedroom, two bathroom home stood on 2.9 acres of land, just what we thought we needed for a family of three. Sitting around the kitchen table enjoying a cup of coffee, the owner shared more information about the house and ended her speech with the words we were waiting to hear. "Our family dog goes with the sale of the house." Alan and I looked at each other and in our hearts thanked God for His faithfulness, thanked God for His sign, thanked God for our new house that we now call HOME! There was a lot of work to be done in minor repairs and painting, but in no time at all this house became a home filled with the love of God.

Chapter Nine
A GENTLE SOUL

Alan became associate pastor in a local church near our home and it was at this church that I met Sherri for the first time. She was a single lady who lived in Grand Ledge who had recently lost her driver's license due to health issues. Sherri wanted to continue attending church here in Nashville with the body of believers that had become her Christian family, but had no one to drive her the 54 miles round trip which took 34 minutes each way. At the beginning of the service, the pastor asked the congregation if anyone would be willing to drive for Sherri, but no one stood up. At the close of the same service, the pastor asked once again for someone to drive for Sherri every Sunday. No one moved. The next thing I remember, I was standing. To this day I have no idea how that happened! I did not know Sherri, but God knew Sherri and that was all that mattered. God had a plan unfolding that would be a blessing to both of us and glorify his Holy name. So it was that for the next year every Sunday, I would drive for "Miss Daisy". Sherri had a great sense of humor and had me laughing in no time at her quick and funny stories.

For the first few Sundays, I would drive four times a day from Nashville to Grand Ledge and back to Nashville first for the morning service and then do it again for the evening service. On one of those Sundays, Sherri invited me to meet her parents after church to have lunch. She didn't tell me it was a birthday luncheon for her father Fred. All but one of her siblings, Greg, were there to celebrate this wonderful man's birthday. Fred's dry humor had us all laughing in no time. I could understand where Sherri got her great sense of humor. Cathy, Sherri's mum and her sisters Jane and Debbie and sister-in-law Ronda had catered for an army. I had not seen so much food in one place since the fiestas we had enjoyed on Saipan. Sherri's brothers, Mike and Joe, made sure everyone had a soft drink in hand so we could toast the birthday boy.

My tummy was rumbling from the smell of all the delicious food covering the dining room table. I had not eaten since early morning. I leaned over to Sherri and quietly asked does your family pray before they eat? She said, "Not normally, Miss Elly."

I said, "Well, they will now." Aloud I said, "Let's hold hands and pray before we eat." Somewhat taken aback they all gathered close and held hands as I led them in a prayer of thankfulness so we could get on with eating. We spent the best part of the afternoon eating all the delicious food and happily chatting. I felt honored to have been invited and thankful for the opportunity to get to know this beautiful family.

Driving all those miles on Sundays was becoming mentally and physically exhausting. I asked my husband, Alan, if Sherri could come to our home between services. He agreed. How happy this made her! She showed her appreciation by bringing us home cooked Sunday meals. After eating, Alan would "relax" in his easy chair. Once he was snoring softly, Sherri would tell me about things that were important to her. I listened carefully as she shared some of her background. God made a way for Sherri to open up to me. She surprised herself because she was a very private person. She kept most everything in her heart to protect her feelings from being hurt. As I learned to listen with my heart and not my ears, it struck me just how much she loved the Lord. Little did I know that God was at work in both of our hearts and spirits building and binding something beautiful in this friendship.

I began to see many parallels between our lives as we talked over the weeks and months that followed. She had lost a lot of schooling due to health reasons. I had lost much schooling also. We both had suffered from low self-esteem. She had been an angry young woman, so had I. She even told me of a time she was so angry she thought about knifing someone. I sat back and looked at my new friend, finding it very hard to believe this gentle soul could be anything but gentle. She was a rough diamond that Jesus saw beauty in, so was I. We had both been raised in non-Christian families. We had both found the Lord later in life. She longed to serve the Lord with all her heart and soul and mind and so did I.

Sherri had zero regrets after she was born again into the family of God. God changed her from the inside out. "I will love and serve Him until He calls me home," she said. It was the desire of Sherri's heart to attend Bible School. She believed that Jesus' name and mission were the same. He came to save the lost. That meant us! We had been so lost for a very long time. Sherri already knew that I had completed a discipleship training school with YWAM even though I had limited education. So she talked to me about feeling unqualified to be a Bible student. I reminded Sherri that Jesus does not call the qualified, He qualifies the called. I reminded her of what I remind myself daily. Walking with Jesus is a daily walk. Talking with Jesus is a daily talk. Living for Jesus and sharing with others what a difference inviting Jesus into your heart has made is a daily opportunity we need to grab hold of. God's love restores all things into their proper place. God's love is a love so real, so fresh, so absorbing, so satisfying, who could ask for more?

Over the years of our friendship Sherri spent a great deal of time in the hospital due to her health issues. She and I spent quality time reading and sharing the word of God together often at her hospital bedside. She always seemed in a positive mood despite the hospital routine. Yet every time she went into the hospital to stay a small part of her was fearful. She smiled and told me that was her human part, we both laughed. I read encouraging comments to reassure her that God was still in control no matter what. Dark fears flee in the light of God's presence, I read. Faith is the best antidote for fear.

"Sherri, God has you here for a reason and while you are here allow God to use you for His glory. You are in a world of darkness that needs the light of Christ. You are His channel through which His light and love can shine. You are ministering without even trying." This put a smile on her sweet little face.

She never asked for anything. She never complained about anything. I knew what she needed from me was acceptance, love and support. I would often find her singing to the Lord on my hospital visits. Sherri loved to sing unto God. She sang from a heart overflowing with gratitude for His amazing grace, His forgiveness, His mercy and His unconditional love. "Praise is a song of a soul set free," she said with a twinkle in her eye. "Jesus is the hope that calms life's storms. In worship I am in His presence, and not focused on my overwhelming situation."

Sherri had her heart fully open to God and it was the soil of her heart where God planted the seed of His word to flourish. "My problems can never exhaust God's provision," she told me. "He is and will always be everything I will ever need. My prayer needs I bring to God daily as I worship him in spirit and in truth and am reminded that faith is the key to answered prayer. I hold on to Jesus my Savior and he holds on to me. How wonderful to know that he will never leave me or forsake me!" (Deuteronomy 31:8.)

God did call this sweet soul home in October 2015. I received a phone call at two in the morning from Ronda to tell me that a car crash had claimed this gentle soul's life. Heartbroken yet thankful, I gave this sad moment into the hands of Jesus. I was sad that I would not see her again this side of heaven, thankful that we will be reunited at the coming of Christ. My husband Alan held me as I cried myself to sleep.

Abundant Life Fellowship Ministries hosted a Celebration of Life service in Sherri's honor. This service was well attended by all that loved her. I think of her often, grateful for the blessing of her friendship.

For you Sherri,
  Sherri, you had a heart of gold, now you have a crown to match,
  God rewarded his good and faithful servant.
  Gonna miss your contagious laugh and your unconditional love.

When your beautiful heart stopped beating,
My heart just broke in two,
Knowing that here on earth,
There will never be another like you.

Many days and in many ways I miss her beautiful, caring ways, yet I am thankful that God's word tells me in I Thessalonians 4:17 that we will be caught up together with them in the clouds to meet the Lord in the air. In John 14:1-3 the Bible talks about the place that is being made ready for the believers in Christ. Jesus says, "I go to prepare a place for you, I will come again and will take you to myself, that where I am you may be also." So Sherri and I will one day be together again in the presence of Almighty God forever.

COME LEAN ON ME

Chapter Ten
A PRECIOUS MOMENT IN TIME

Some time before Sherri died, my son Matthew taught her to shoot. He was so patient when he taught her how to hold the gun, aim and shoot. She felt vulnerable because she lived alone. Her eyesight was starting to fail because of her diabetes and she wanted to learn how to protect herself. Matt wanted her to have the confidence to learn and so on the day he taught her to shoot he took time to play around with the targets until he found the right distance and style target that would give her the confidence to practice. However many times she missed he never belittled her or got angry. He would only move or change the target to the right kind so she could see what she was shooting at. He even went with her when she purchased her first firearm to help her get the best one for her. Even though he was every inch a peacemaker he knew we lived in a fallen world. Even though he believed in God's protection, he also believed in the right to bear arms.

Even while inside the womb Matthew was patient. He was very comfortable where he was. One day near the end of my pregnancy, to try and encourage him to come out, I took a very hot bath. Matt decided it was too hot. He became very active. I invited Alan and his mum into the bathroom to enjoy the antics. He pushed one little foot up and Alan's mother reached over and pushed it down, up popped the other foot, just as if he was trying to cool off. But he still stayed put coming into this world three weeks after his due date just like the rest of his siblings. He was also kind, bursting into this world after only one pain, nine pounds nine ounces of all boy.

I had prayed for a boy to complete our family. It just seemed like two boys and two girls would make it right. Alan had even bought a little two-piece white baby outfit with blue trim and hung it in the kitchen to remind me of the faithfulness of God. Whenever I doubted that God was going to give me the son I desired I was to look at the outfit and remember, *"If you believe, you will receive whatever you ask for in prayer."* (Matthew 21:22)

How blessed we were to have this precious son! In the delivery room, I looked up at Alan's face and saw the joy unspeakable fill every part of him. He looked down at the precious child now lying peacefully in his arms. I leaned into them and Alan placed the sweetest kiss on the top of my head as if to say thank you. While embracing his family right there in the delivery room, Alan prayed to God out loud. He thanked God for the safe arrival of this child. He thanked God for keeping me safe through the birthing process. He gave this child back to God in prayer and asked God to fill this child with the fullness of Christ in every way, every day. We were moved to tears as the Spirit of God filled our hearts with a peace that passes all understanding.

I clearly remember the day about a year later when Dee, his oldest sister, had taken Matthew out in his umbrella stroller for a walk in the beautiful warm afternoon and when they returned he was fast asleep. I put his stroller right next to the unplugged washing machine in full view of the rest of the family as we sat eating. All of a sudden the steel vice that Alan had purchased earlier that day and had placed on top of the washing machine, fell. It stopped right beside Matthew's left ear yet never touched the sleeping baby. It sat there in midair. Matthew remained fast asleep. Alan and I looked at each other without saying a word, then Alan got up from the table and walked over to the stroller where he carefully lifted the steel vice from beside Matthew's ear and placed it back on top of the unplugged washing machine. No I cannot explain it to you. No, I have no understanding of how it fell, or why it never crushed our one year old's skull killing him. However, I can share with you this truth, God offers his pure and selfless love through the use of his angels. I was convinced at that point that God had already appointed His angel to watch over Matthew. Psalm 91:11-12 "For He will command His angels concerning you to guard you in all your ways. They will lift you up in their hands so that you will not strike your foot against a stone."

After moving many times and living in different cultures, we finally settled in Michigan in the year 2001. Matthew attended Maple Valley High School and graduated from there a happy young man. As the Michigan seasons changed I watched as my men became agitated to get out of the house to fish, hunt and just hang out as father and son over the barbecue pit. They both loved the outdoor life and as I watched them interact with each other, it made my heart so very thankful to God for this precious gift of family. It didn't matter to them if they were doing yard work or fishing, both had a great sense of humor and found much to laugh at with each other. I even overheard Matthew say to his father once, "I don't need more to be thankful for, I just need to be more thankful." The spirit of God was at work in Matthew's heart.

One day he came and told us he wanted to be baptized. This decision had the three of us hugging and crying with joy. Less than a month later his father and I had the privilege of watching Matthew get baptized. We were so happy to see our son take action on his decision making an outward declaration to an inward commitment to Christ in the cool waters of St. Mary's Lake on a beautiful, sunny afternoon.

Some years later Matthew talked with us about joining the armed services. He wanted to do something worthwhile with his life. He had a strong sense of morality and a strong protective streak and with the war on terror going on he felt he wanted to be part of the team that fought against it. Army life had been part of his father's and grandfather's lives, so Matt wanted to follow suit in joining the Army Infantry.

I was not in favor of Matt going into the forces. I was worried that his Christian life would suffer. Like any mother, I was afraid for my son's life, as soldiers were being sent overseas to fight the war on terror. But his father thought it would be a good thing and Matthew joined up. The time came for him to leave on his adventure. We watched as he graduated from boot camp and was sent to the California desert for more training.

Four long years of separation took its toll on our family in different ways. I had to really lean on God to believe the angel that He had assigned to care for Matt as an infant would indeed care for him now as a soldier. We prayed for Matt daily asking God for protection: protection of Matt's heart for Christ as well as his body. Writing back and forth gave Alan and me some understanding of Army life and the changes that were taking place in Matt.

Matthew's return home was a family celebration around our kitchen table, with stories that would curl your hair. Having our son home safe brought happy smiles to everyone's faces. I had leaned on God to protect my son and God came through. I found myself on my knees in thankful prayer to God for keeping our son safe.

Since Matthew had lived with strict routine for the last four years he felt he needed to have his own space and even though I wanted him close and living with us Matthew rented a home of his own. It was a beautiful log cabin high on a hill within a five-minute drive from us. This beautiful cabin was perfect in every way for his needs.

Alan and I would often invite ourselves over to find Matthew outside doing woodwork. One time we were there he was making a beautiful six-foot long dinner table and two benches. Another time we were there he was working on a solid wood headboard. Matthew was a gifted young man who put this gift to good use.

One day Alan and I were taking some left over food to our son and as we drove up the long, steep curling driveway we noticed Matthew was not alone. Standing next to him by the wooden workbench was a beautiful woman. Call it mother's instinct, but my heart leapt within me. I turned to my husband and said, "There is the women that will one day be Matthew's wife."

Alyssa was introduced to us and Matt shared his food with her while still standing outside. She had very red rosy cheeks from being out in the cold. Dressed in winter camouflage only her sweet little face was visible, but the tenderness in her voice told this mother's heart all I needed to know.

I was so proud of Matt because he had secured a job working nights at Pennock Hospital in Hastings, Michigan in the emergency department. Long twelve hour night shifts found him sleeping most of the next day ready to do it all again. Matthew loved his work. Matthew loved his co-workers. He was completely fulfilled in this chosen career. To have a shorter drive home when tired, he felt a need to move closer to his place of employment. Although not happy, I understood why Matthew chose to move into Hastings.

His love of the outdoors would occasionally bring him to our land to hunt. He loved venison and wanted to fill his freezer with this meat. Matthew would often stop by the house for a quick hello after a couple of hours of early morning hunting before heading to his own house to rest.

On weekends when his daddy was home Alan would ask Matt how things were going at work. We sat in silence and listened to true stories of the great work that the Pennock ER did in caring for the sick and needy. No names were ever mentioned, but I watched as my son took great delight in sharing how he, as part of a team, made a great difference in the lives of others.

One of Matt's de-stressors from work was fishing. On one of these fishing trips I was invited to go along. I packed for a week including a very large sport umbrella with a bungee cord. As Matt and Alan loaded all my things, they looked at each other and smiled, but I knew what that smile meant. "Why do you need an umbrella mum?" Matt asked. "There is not a cloud in the sky."

"You never know," came my reply.

When we got to Wall Lake the sun was still beating down pretty hot so I attached the umbrella to Alan's fishing chair so that he was shaded and went to catch bait for both men. Later in the day our dear friend, Uncle Blas, as Matt called him, came to join us for the delicious fried chicken and rice I had packed for the day.

Wall Lake was a perfect place to fish. It was so quiet, so picturesque, so calming. I felt my body relax from the rush of the day. Under the water dogfish swam in the hundreds and these were what Alan and Matt were fishing for. The spiny dog fish has dorsal fins, but no anal fin, and dark green spots along its back. The dogfish poses little threat to humans, but if it is not handled properly, the spines on its dorsal fins can give a harmful wound. These aggressive fish are part of the shark family. These fish gave Alan and Matt the challenge they loved.

After lunch, Matt needed to use the restroom. Uncle Blas told him to go to his house since it was nearby. Matt had his bait in the water so he laid his rod down carefully and asked his father to grab it if a fish took the bait. Matt started walking away and as he passed me his rod was pulled into the water. Alan gave a scream. I saw my son run past me and dive into the water. Moments later Matt was reeling in his catch while still in the water. Once he was close enough to the dock, Matt handed Alan his rod so that he could climb back onto the dock. Once on the dock Alan handed back the rod.

The water came alive with activity. Matt's veins came alive with adrenaline as he reeled and pulled at his opponent who pulled back. Alan and I were cheering. Uncle Blas was cheering. Suddenly everything was calm. The fish got free. The fighting was done and the fish had won! Matthew needed the bathroom and clean clothes!

Matt was determined to try again, so later in the afternoon we all sat together as dark clouds started to fill the sky. Uncle Blas went home to rest when all of a sudden, out of nowhere the clouds opened up and the rain started to fall. Matt and I huddled under the umbrella with Alan. The wind picked up so much that Matt had to help me hold on to the handle of the umbrella. The wind and the rain increased with such a mighty force that it took the shade of the umbrella completely off its frame. We watched it as it floated onto the water. What a sight we were, standing under only the umbrella frame still holding to the handle as the rain lashed us from all sides. In no time at all the freak storm was gone, and the sunshine reappeared. "Good job you brought the umbrella, Mum," Matt said with a glint in his eye and a tease in his voice. As a family we made a memory to cherish, to tell again, to laugh at, to remember.

Over the three years that Matthew and Alyssa dated, I noticed my son's heart soften. I saw him open and close the car door for the woman he loved. I heard the softness in his voice when they were together at my house playing family games around the table. At his house I would ask him a question but before he answered me he said, "Let me check with Alyssa first and I will get back with you." Her love had made a strong impact in his heart. Over time, her love healed his pain, and it was her love that totally healed the scars of his past failed relationships. The bond between Matthew and Alyssa became stronger and stronger as time went on.

One day the two of them came to our property to go mushroom hunting on the land behind our house. Alan and I were sitting on the front deck enjoying a nice cup of coffee when they emerged from the woods. Alyssa had the biggest smile on her beautiful face as she came walking up to us. She held out her left hand and sitting on her ring finger was Matthew's promise of marriage. Hugs, hugs and more hugs were given and received. This beautiful soul whose love had captured my son's heart was going to be my new daughter. I could not have been more blessed. It was a precious moment in time. Matthew and Alyssa told us their wedding date would be May 4, 2018.

A few days later Matt asked me to go fishing with him. I was pleasantly surprised that he had invited only me to share his day. It was mother and son time that I had longed for and now looked forward to. I met him at Wall Lake and out we went in his little fishing boat. Sitting under a clear blue sky, Matt opened up. He asked me several deep spiritual questions. I was so proud he felt safe to ask me and so proud he was searching for answers to life's questions. I was glad he wanted to be a good spiritual leader to his intended.

Out of nowhere he told me he needed to use the restroom, and did I have any toilet tissue with me. Matt steered the boat into a jungle like tree formation and disappeared for a short while. When he returned I asked him, as any concerned mother would, how he managed to clean himself up without toilet paper. A cheeky smile ran across his face. "I used my boxer shorts he said, but I still have a tummy ache so I better not get into the boat just yet." He waited. I waited. Not long and he disappeared for the second time. I was sitting in the little boat lost in my thoughts when my son reappeared smiling. "Do you like my new look?" he asked. I burst into laughter. The ripping sound that I had heard was Matt tearing off the short sleeves of his t-shirt to clean himself up. What a wonderful day we had together. We never caught any fish, but that was all right. We had a memory to laugh at and to cherish forever.

The LORD is close to the
brokenhearted and saves those who
are crushed in spirit.

— Psalm 34:18 (NIV)

COME LEAN ON ME

Chapter Eleven
FAREWELL SMALL FRY

It was Tuesday, October 24. I had finished making Alan's birthday cake for the next day. I texted Matthew and Rebecca, our daughter, who now lived in the USA, that daddy's surprise birthday cake was finished and ready. The two children had agreed to come over in time for the party the next day.

Naomi, my best friend of thirty years was with me at my house when the phone rang. As I said hello, the person on the other end said four words that tightened my chest and made my mouth dry.

"Your son is dead."

I stood there, phone in hand waiting for the words to make sense to me. I repeated the words back to the caller, "MY SON IS DEAD?" The next voice I heard was Alyssa's sobbing uncontrollably. "Elly, Matthew is gone." I asked her where she was and she said on her way to Pennock Hospital. I heard motion behind me as Naomi got together our coats and shoes. I grabbed my house keys and Naomi drove the fifteen minutes to the hospital. While she was driving, I called Alan at work and left a message for him to call me back as soon as possible on my cell phone. I phoned Matthew's sister, Rebecca, and told her to get to the hospital as soon as she could. By the sound of my voice she knew something was really wrong. "Mum! What's wrong? Mum! What's happened?"

I tried to find words. Not just any words, but words that would be the kindest possible for her to hear that would give her the least amount of pain. I could hear the fear in her voice. I felt it way down in the pit of my stomach. "Bexs, it's your brother," I tried to say as calmly as I could. "There has been an accident." She was pleading for the truth. The truth was her baby brother had been killed. Rebecca's scream filled my ears and my heart broke for the pain I could hear in her sobbing. Over and over in my mind I repeated the cry for God's mercy. Devlin had died. David had died. Now I pleaded for God to spare my son Matthew's life, but it was not to be. God took our son Matthew home one day before his father's birthday, and seven months before his wedding to the love of his life, Alyssa.

My greatest weakness was not asking God for his strength. God hears even the faintest cry for help. I know that God's love does not keep me from life's trials, but sees me through them. And through them I would know He was there.

Naomi stayed by my side as we found the room I thought my son was in, but when I opened the door, Alyssa was in the bed brokenhearted. "Where is my son?" I asked her.

She was not able to answer, because she was in shock. I turned and left the room to see Alan walking down the corridor. We fell into each other's arms crying. Bexs, Jason her husband and their two daughters, Shia, 17 and Jaysona-Skye, 7 were coming up behind Alan. We all went into a waiting room and I tried to explain to Alan the little I knew.

The friends of the hospital came bringing light refreshments, but no one ate. The room was decorated with the words, "God's peace, love and hope" written in large letters on the wall. Naomi helped me fill out some paperwork before Alan said it was best for us to go home for tomorrow would soon be here. I hugged Naomi and thanked her for all her help. I gave my daughter and her family soft kisses goodbye then Alan and I drove home in silence. Not once did I think to find out where my son was. Not once did I think to go to the accident site. I believe this was God's way of protecting my heart, protecting my emotions. This was too similar a scenario to what I had experienced years ago. That night neither Alan nor I slept.

We later learned what had happened. Matthew had slept well into the afternoon because he worked the previous night. Alyssa normally checked the mail, but had gotten behind and forgot to check it, so when Matt was up and ready for work he went to the end of his driveway to check the mail. He never knew what hit him.

Matthew died from multiple blunt force injuries sustained when a pickup truck that had left the road hit and killed him instantly. The young driver had been distracted. This was a tragic accident that never needed to happen. I took comfort in bringing to mind something I had read days before. No life is more secure than a life surrendered to God. Matthew had done just that. He lived to please God. God's unconditional love for him made it possible by faith in Christ Jesus to break the strongholds of fear of tomorrow.

Talking with Naomi some time later she shared with me a picture she received when the phone call had come about Matthew's death. She saw Matthew's earthly body lying on the ground, then Matthew's spirit body got up and walked away from his earthly body.

II Corinthians 5:8 says absent from the body, present with the Lord.

The day after, Alan and I met with Alyssa at the Girrbach Funeral Home in Hastings, Michigan to talk over funeral arrangements for Matthew. The following Monday, October 30, 2017 at 9 A.M. the Celebration of Life service was held, Dr. David MacDonald officiated. Three hundred and fifty family and friends came to pay their respects to this wonderful young man. Alyssa's father and Matthew's father both shared a few words. Matthew's niece, Shia, also shared from a heart that will greatly miss an uncle she loved. Matthew was laid to rest at Fort Custer National Cemetery with full military honors. Abundant Life Fellowship Ministries in Nashville catered a wonderful lunch for everyone to enjoy.

Alan returned to work as a substance addiction counselor, brokenhearted. I watched him as he pulled himself out of bed each workday morning. I watched him slowly eat less and less. Don't cook any more in the evenings he said. I will eat at work. But I later found out he didn't eat at work. I watched him as he lost interest in the hobby he loved best, fishing. I listened as he cried himself to sleep every night curled in a fetal position. I prayed asking God to fill Alan with His peace, His grace, and His love.

I made an appointment with a grief counselor in Hastings and we went together. I had heard that Ascension Counseling, Hastings dealt with families struggling with grief. Erik Olson made us very welcome and sat listening as Alan shared the pain he felt in the unexpected loss of our son, Matthew.

Tears filled Alan's eyes as he shared the many things he would not be experiencing now. He would not stand beside his son on his wedding day and watch him become a husband. He would not watch him become a father and carry on the family's name. Erik was deeply moved as he watched and listened with compassion to the man sitting across from him.

They say that time is the great healer, but time was not going to let us heal without constant reminders of that painful day.

Matthew had not left a will so it was decided that I, as next of kin, would be the personal representative of our son's estate. A close friend of the family, Eugenia took my hand and helped lead me through a long day of filing and filling out paperwork with the Hastings Probate Court. I was emotionally overwhelmed with all that needed to be addressed on that day. I was extremely thankful for the tremendous support of Eugenia.

Claudia, the probate clerk, was very sympathetic to my emotional state. She drafted the necessary papers for me to sign. I paid the one hundred and eighty-seven dollars filing fee and was told to check back in a week to see if the Letters of Authority were ready for me to pick up. I needed these in order to close out Matthew's accounts and deal with his estate.

A few days later Naomi went with me to the Hastings Reminder office to post in the Banner newspaper, a notice to his creditors. I paid out more money. After lunch we went to see the Hastings police chief, Jeff Pratt. He welcomed us into his office and listened as I explained why I was there. Since the police were involved, I wanted to know if there was a report about the accident to give me better understanding of what had happened that dreadful night. I'm sure I saw tears in his eyes as he witnessed how brokenhearted I was. "We will do everything in our power to see that justice is served," he said. After a warm handshake we left his office.

On November 17, 2017 I received a call to say that the Letter of Authority was ready to pick up. The next day Naomi took me to the courthouse. Once I had the Letter of Authority in my hand I started addressing Matthew's outstanding bills. Twelve thousand dollars later all creditors were paid. Matthew's funeral bill was paid. Now to face the next emotional hurdle.

On December 26, 2017, I received a phone call from Chief Pratt saying the Barry County's prosecutor's office would be calling me soon. I received a phone call shortly afterwards from Josh Carter, assistant prosecutor of the Barry County prosecutor's office saying the young man that killed our son was being charged with, Moving Violation Causing Death. On Friday, January 4, 2018 Alan and I were asked to meet with Josh Carter and the prosecuting attorney, Julie A. Nakfoor-Pratt, at their office. Also in the office was Sunny Anderson, victim rights representative. Julie shared an outline of the case and time frame and gave Alan and me a copy of most the police report blacking out identifying information not relevant to us. Sunny said she would keep us updated to any court hearings pending. I liked her warm, compassionate smile. She was true to her word. We received a letter dated January 26, 2018 informing us of the February 13, 2018 pretrial should we want to attend.

Leaning on God, I asked my husband to pray with me. We opened up God's word to find comfort in these words, "God is our refuge and strength, a very present help in trouble," Psalm 46:1 (KJV) Not just a help, but a VERY present help. I took courage in that, knowing that courage is not the absence of fear, but the mastery of it.

The night before the pretrial found Alan and me unable to sleep. We both knew what the other one was thinking: tomorrow we will come face to face with the young man that took the life of our son.

Judge Michael L. Schipper sat and listened as the young offender pleaded not guilty. NOT GUILTY! How could he plead not guilty? He was the one driving the pickup truck that left the road and struck our son, killing him instantly. He was the only person in the truck. He was the one that was at the scene when the police arrived. He was the one taken into custody by the police after being taken to the hospital for a Breathalyzer test that proved negative. He was the one out on parole. I prayed hard. I prayed that God would intervene on our behalf and keep us focused on the Savior and not on the situation. I prayed that God would protect the hearts that had been broken by this terrible tragedy. I prayed for God's love to cover us all.

Alyssa, her sisters and parents together with Alan, our daughter Rebecca, me and our close friend Naomi were horrified at his denial of the truth that he was actually guilty. The judge asked the young offender if he wanted a lawyer. He said yes and the next court date was set for February 27, 2018. The young man didn't make eye contact with us. He was led in and out of the courtroom in chains.

At the second court hearing the same family members attended only to hear the same plea repeated. Not Guilty. And a trial date was set.

We received another letter dated March 1, 2018 informing us of another court hearing set for May 1, 2018. Again Alan and I went. Again Judge Michael L Schipper was presiding. Again the young offender pleaded not guilty. A new date was set right there in the courtroom for May 10th, 2018. As before he said not guilty. This was going nowhere!

Why was he pleading not guilty time and again? Why couldn't he own up and take responsibility for his actions and spare himself this kind of embarrassment. Did he like the attention? Was it about drawing out the pain of those affected by the senseless death of a beautiful soul? I started to hate him. I started to want him dead like my son. I wanted him to suffer, and cry with the deepest pain imaginable, that of the loss of a child. I wanted him to know how badly he had hurt me. I wanted him to have no peace, no happiness ever. I wanted him to die. Bitterness rose up within me, all I could think of was how to get back at him for the loss I felt. My time with God suffered badly. I tried to stay focused on God. I tried to read his Holy Word. I tried to pray. I tried to worship. But I didn't try hard enough.

A phone call came to inform us that a new court date had been set: May 14, 2018. We were asked to have a victim's impact statement ready should we need it. Alan said he would not say anything. He asked me to represent our family.

I sat at my computer and put together a letter that was full of anger. I knew this was wrong of me, so I destroyed it. A day or so later, I sat at the computer again, this time the letter I wrote was full of blame, so I destroyed that one too. The third and final letter that I wrote was what I knew God expected of me and what my son would have me say. As the mother of Matthew, I choose to walk in forgiveness towards this young man.

As part of my victim's impact statement during the court hearing I was able to read out part of a personal letter that Matthew had sent to me when he was serving in the military. I read out loud to the entire courtroom these words:

"Hi everyone. If you are hearing this letter than I am absent from the body and present with the Lord. I'm just so darn glad I lived a life so full of love, joy and amazing friends. I'm lucky to say I have zero regrets. I spent every ounce of energy I had living life to the fullest. I love you all and thank you for this awesome life. My energy, my love, my laughter, those incredible memories, it's all here with you now. Please don't think of me with pity or sadness, instead smile, knowing that we had a blast together and that time was amazing. I have always tried the best I knew how to make those around me smile and laugh. So please don't dwell on my passing, instead laugh at the happy memories we made together and the great fun we shared."

As I closed my victim's impact statement I was aware of the silence that had filled the courtroom. I heard the soft sound of sobbing as these words hit hard into the soft hearts of many listening. My husband who had once said he would not speak, stood up next and shared his thoughts and feelings. What I wasn't aware of was that his heart would speak, not his lips.

"We forgive you," Alan said, as he turned to look at the young offender facing him just a short reach away. "I do not believe you intended to take a life. My son Matthew was a man of forgiveness. Go make a good life for yourself. We wish you the very best." Alan finished with these words, "I pray you will find the Lord as your personal savior and turn your life around and do good with the rest of your life."

When given the chance to speak, the young offender pleaded "no contest" in the death of our son Matthew, sparing us a full jury trial and having to relive that terrible day all over again. Alan thanked him for his plea.

The young man was given fines and costs of $500.00. County jail - 365 days, to be served forthwith and run concurrent with prison time being served now. In my words, this habitual offender had gotten off scot free with the taking of a beautiful life so full of potential and promise.

Seven long months later it was over. Now to try and rebuild what was left of our hearts. Now to come before the Lord for cleansing of body, soul and spirit. Now it was time to work through all that had taken place since that very sad day October 24, 2017.

Alan and I took some comfort in reading the cards and emails written about our son. Alex Hill wrote, "The quality of Matthew's life is most easily seen through the incredible connections he made with people around him. His kindness and warm heart brought all types of people together and genuinely made others happy. I'm honored to have gotten to know him, mostly through those close to him and I know that his memory will shine brightly in everyone's heart forever."

Shannon Monroe wrote, "He was an amazing person and will be greatly missed. He had the biggest heart; we all called him our big teddy bear at work. He always went out of his way to make sure we were all happy and laughing when we worked together."

As comforting as these words from people were, it was God's Word that gave me the greatest comfort. The hunger for spending time with God was returning to me. There was a fire burning in my soul. My morning devotional time went from a quick prayer to extended time listening to His Word and praising His name. God's Word was penetrating my soul and making me whole. Slowly I was healing. I am not saying that every day was a victory day in my emotions, but the power and presence of Almighty God carried me through the dark waters of pain to see His light revealed in my walk of faith.

In hope of eternal life, which God, that cannot lie, promised before the world began;

— Titus 1:2 (KJV)

COME LEAN ON ME

Chapter Twelve
UNENDING
FAMILY LOVE

I first met Cathy while volunteering in Nashville at the Methodist Church helping to give out food boxes to needy families. Cathy loved people. She loved to make people feel special. Cathy was always looking for ways to help improve the quality of life for those she met. It was coming to the end of the summer and the food distribution. Cathy approached Naomi and me and asked us if we would be willing to volunteer for another community project. We both said yes.

Cathy marched us over to the Maple Valley Alternative Education building across the road and introduced us to the principal, Chris Parkinson. He needed someone to set up a daycare at the school so that young parents could return to school and take part in the photography class offered. We were told this would be one day a week. Word spread like wild fire about the campus daycare and young parents started coming back to school full time. Within that first year, Naomi and I had 19 children under five Monday to Friday.

The Lord blessed this work, after all it was He that put us there. Cathy would often stop by to check how things were going and to see if we needed her help with anything. I was very thankful to God for this opportunity to serve Him in this wonderful and meaningful way. I was also very thankful to Cathy for believing in us and for the way that she would often turn up with goodies for the daycare or the families that we served. For me this was a precious moment in time; a time when I felt the hand of God leading, guiding and directing my life, and in so doing giving my heart fulfillment in ministry.

My friendship with Cathy grew and soon I was going over to her house to visit with her. We talked about many things and soon she discovered that Alan and Matt loved fishing. So did her husband Blas. It was fishing season and so she invited them to come and use their dock and boat to fish Wall Lake. A friendship between the men grew as well. Alan, Matt and Blas would sit silently for hours as their poles sat in the water.

Becoming family instead of just friends to Blas and Cathy came naturally to us all. They included my family in many of their family activities. One such event was watching the Fourth of July firework celebrations from their Pontoon boat while sitting comfortably in the darkness of the night. Another time we joined with the family to celebrate Blas' birthday. Alan and I were the only non-blood relatives attending, but you never would have known. The love and respect between the men grew deep and strong.

Cathy and Blas were devoted to one and other in every way and their love mentored my relationship with my husband. Blas took my head off one day because I addressed my husband in what he considered a rude way by calling Alan my old man. Blas said that I should always call my husband by the highest level of admiration I knew. Blas always addressed his wife as his bride, even though they had been married for forty eight years. She was his life. He was hers. They were so very connected.

There was always a warm welcome in their cottage with plenty of food and happy fellowship. I watched as family activities surrounded this loving couple. They were always with their children or grandchildren. One day I went to visit Cathy only to find Blas at home alone. He made us a lovely cup of coffee and we sat at the table chatting. I asked him to tell me something about him that I did not know. He told me of how he took care of his daughter and grandchildren through the horrible illness and passing of his wonderful son-in-law. Family meant everything to him. He held his family in high regard. He told me that family is God's gift that we are to always treasure. Through Blas, God was teaching me the value of family. Blas told me to always take care of the less fortunate and share what you have with others if at all possible for you never know when you will be the one in need.

In April of 2018 Blas became very ill with the cancer he had been battling with for the past several years. It slowly robbed his body of strength. But his sense of humor was as sharp as ever. Four days before God called Blas home, Alan and I went to visit him at his request. While sitting on his bed, Blas asked Alan and me to officiate at his home going. Alan took Blas's hand tenderly in his and asked Blas one question. "Have you received the Lord Jesus Christ as your personal Savior?" With a warm and grateful smile opening up on this dear friend's face, he replied. "YES, I HAVE!" Then Blas took my hand and with a twinkle in his eye said to me, "Elly, keep your part short," then we all laughed knowing how much I love to talk. The peace of God was very evident in his tone as we continued to fellowship for a while. Four days later this dear soul joined his Savior in heaven more alive than he ever was on earth. During his celebration of life service seven lost souls were brought into the kingdom of God.

Cathy and I continue to be close friends to this day. She still serves the community around her. She never gives up. She is such an inspiration to me. She leads her family with strong Christian values and principles. Her love of God and commitment to Him is what keeps her going strong. I admire her strength.

Chapter Thirteen

A GOLDEN OPPORTUNITY

In the spring of 2017, God used a beautiful lady doctor to speak right into my spirit. I had gone to see Dr. Tina Stanford because I was having difficulty reading small print up close. I had never met her before. She welcomed me into the Battle Creek office and began looking into my eyes. During my first visit with her I could sense something different about her that made me feel peaceful in my spirit.

I asked Tina if she was a Christian. She smiled ever so sweetly, held her head up high, and said, "Yes I am." From that point on I started to talk about the Savior we both loved and served. When Tina was close to ending the exam, she asked me a question. "What do you want the Lord to do for you?"

I was somewhat taken aback, but just for a second or two. "Well," I said, "I have been seeking the Lord for an opportunity to travel throughout America and share the good news of the gospel with anyone that will listen."

"No. That's not it," she said. Not understanding where this cute little blond was coming, I waited. Then I told Tina that for some time I had been thinking about writing a book for the glory of God.

"That's it!" she said, "that is what you have to do." She became animated. "I saw your appearance in my devotions this morning. You have to follow the calling on your life. The desire of your heart to honor and please God." Dr. Tina told me she would contact a friend who was both an author and proof-reader and this person would help me with my book.

Tina told me to pray and God would make his will clear. That night just as I was going to sleep, the Holy Spirit touched me and said, "Get up. Find a pencil and paper and write down every word I tell you." In the morning I told my husband what had happened. Alan said to take the day and wait on the Lord for His direction for the next step. I did just that. God made it very clear to me that day that I was to write three books: Come Walk With Me, Come Lean on Me, and Come Learn From Me. And I was to pioneer a ministry called Helping Others Prepare for Eternity Ministries, HOPE for short. I saw this as a golden opportunity, a way that God's Word could go where I could not go. That my story of God's abounding grace could touch hearts and bring inner healing as the reader experienced a fresh hope and deeper walk of faith. These three books have become known as the COME series.

I took chapter one to a meeting I had arranged with a godly sister named Debbie Moore. She had written many books guided by the Holy Spirit, so she had a better understanding of what was required. As we sat across the table from each other over lunch, I ate as Debbie started to read the chapter I had given her. I looked up at her every now and then to see her wipe a tear from her eye. When she had finished reading, Debbie said, "I believe this is an anointed work that must be finished and published." With tears still sitting on the lower lids of her eyes she reached her hand across the table and gently laid her hand on mine. "I will help you", she said. "I will stand by your side in daily praying for this work of faith. I believe in you." Her words so tender, so real, so encouraging gave me hope that indeed God had called me and therefore would be with me in this commission for His glory. I set to work soon afterwards. Within three months the manuscript was ready for Debbie to proofread.

As this was a work of faith, I shared with my home church family the project and asked them to pray for this work. The completed project would cost three thousand dollars. I didn't even have three hundred, but I knew who did, God. My ministry partner and best friend of thirty years, Naomi, said we need to trust and not doubt that God will bring in the finances we need.

We prayed asking God to bring in the money needed for this work.

We started a prayer dairy and wrote in it all the needs and blessings that we had. It was encouraging to us to look back over the entries and see how God had answered our prayer requests. It also kept us focused on the call of our ministry. I saw how quickly God answered many of our prayers even though it felt like forever to me. I saw that God was in control and His timing is perfect. He is never in a rush and He is never late.

Since we had a mission road trip already planned, we wanted to take the book with us. This meant we also needed to put a time frame on the total cost required for printing. My home church gave as they could and small gifts were coming in from other friends. However, drawing close to the deadline we still needed two thousand dollars more. It was days before the deadline when I received an envelope containing more than enough to cover all the costs in the strangest way.

The Friday before our deadline my husband, Alan, came home and tripped as he came in the door. It was a door he had come in thousands of times before. Nothing was new, but somehow he tripped and the contents of his work bag spilled out onto the floor. Laying among the jumble was a long white envelope addressed to me. "Oh, sorry, my darling," said Alan. "This letter for you came on Monday and I forgot to give it to you." I held in my hands the answer to our prayers. Now that my friend is, God's faithfulness in action.

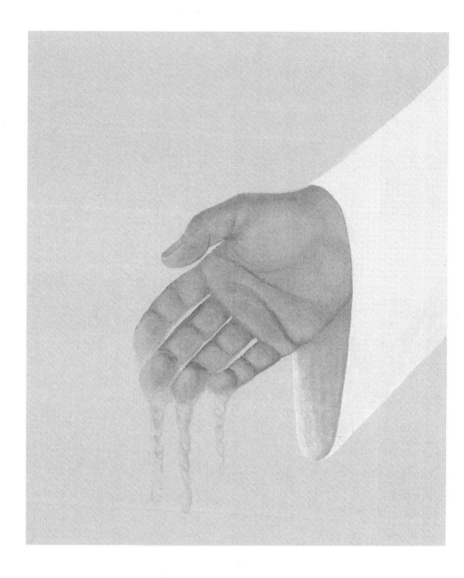

The LORD is close to the brokenhearted and saves those who are crushed in spirit Even there shall thy hand lead me, and thy right hand shall hold me.

— Psalm 139:10 (KJV)

COME LEAN ON ME

Chapter Fourteen
REACHING MILLIONS

With the money in and the book close to being printed, I contacted our mission trip host Jared Okoth, founder of The Lights of the Nations International Ministries, in Jackson, Tennessee to give him the good news. Jared was excited that God had answered our prayers. He told us that his church had been praying for the needs of our ministry and they would be excited to see and hear how God had worked to get the book done so fast. He told us how he had been seeking the Lord on our behalf for open doors of ministries in and around Tennessee and that we had more than enough churches to fill our three-week outreach there. He laughingly asked if we could stay longer. Not this trip we said, but maybe at a later date.

With my husband's blessing, Naomi and I set out for our trip to Tennessee, loaded down with boxes containing books of hope for a hurting world. Jared and his lovely wife Angela hosted our three-week stay in their beautiful home that God had given them. They set a schedule that had us running, but oh it was so worth it.

Apostle Anna Shears and her church family at Temple of Lights Global Church in Southaven, Mississippi invited me to be their guest speaker for a three-day conference. I ministered on "Walking in Forgiveness, Walking in Holiness, Walking in Victory." I shared from personal experience how I had to make a choice to forgive those that hurt me in my past. I had to make a choice that would require me kneeling before the throne of God's unending grace. I had to choose to allow Him to do the much needed soul surgery to free me completely from the lies the enemy of God told me were truth. It was not God's fault that I was wounded in my younger years. I lived in a fallen world. Yet to be honest with you, I did blame Him more than once for the sadness that seemed to follow me through life.

I shared that it wasn't until I became God's child and grew in His knowledge and wisdom that I knew the only freedom I would ever experience would be at the hands of Jesus Christ my Lord and Savior. I shared that forgiving someone that had hurt me was the greatest challenge of my life. When I chose to forgive, and yes it's a choice, I joined those who are not being destroyed by bitterness, anger or other toxic emotions. I asked myself this question. How can I expect God to forgive me if I do not forgive others? I read aloud Luke 6: 27 & 28, "Love your enemies, do good to those who hate you, bless those who curse you, pray for those who mistreat you." Wow! That's a packed couple of verses. I did put those verses into play. I ended day one of the conference with these words found in Psalm 51:10, "Create in me a clean heart oh God, and renew a right spirit within me."

Day two God led me to share about walking in holiness. God reminded me that I am a citizen of heaven and as such my life should reflect my desire to make him first place in every decision. I led this beautiful church family to 2 Timothy 2:15, "Do your best to present yourself to God as one approved, a worker who does not need to be ashamed and who correctly handles the word of truth." I shared that walking in holiness is the best way to honor God.

I also gave them three disadvantages of disobedience. When walking in disobedience to God's will, our testimony of Christ is destroyed. Our spirituality is dead. And our soul is found in the gutter, gasping its last breath because of the separation from the Spirit that gave us life. I reminded this beautiful church family what the letters S. I. N. stand for: Satan Is Near.

I tried to encourage them that God lives in the believer's heart. Our heart is His dwelling place.

Greater is He who is within us, than he who is in the world. Yes, the victory over death and sin is the Lord Jesus Christ. It is He, by invitation, who will inhabit the heart of a soul saved by grace.

I concluded the conference that as believers we are to walk in victory, God's victory, and show that it's His power at work in us and through us that will overcome every attack from the evil one of this world. I know God places high value on His children and His church, therefore we are to uproot and tear down the strongholds of the enemy in the mighty name of Jesus. We are to plant and build Godly values. This can only be done successfully if we lean on God for wisdom, lean on God for direction and lean on God for his power and authority.

I closed out the conference with Romans 16:20a, "The God of peace will soon crush Satan under your feet." Leaning on God is walking in victory. Walking in victory is God's gift to his church, His bride. It's called grace. God's Righteousness At Christ's Expense.

It was such an honor to be invited. God blessed in many ways. Hearts were touched. Hearts were healed. Hearts were set free by the mighty power of a loving and living God. I even kicked off my shoes when I shared the meaning of freedom! What a wonderful welcome we received. This family of God was such a blessing to me personally, and I know they are to God Himself.

Tuesday mornings Naomi and I joined Jared and his wife, Angela, for a time of prayer at Lane College. Together with other pastors we gained insight into the spiritual needs of the college body. This college was founded on Christian principles, but had become worldly. Prayer is the weapon of spiritual warfare that we used to crash the gates of hell and trust for spiritual freedom and renewal for students, staff and faculty. The spirit of God moved in a powerful way during our prayer times together and we left the building feeling very encouraged to know that strongholds were being broken in the lives of the students.

In Cordova, Tennessee, Pastor Babu Thomas and his church family welcomed us with open arms as I ministered on Psalm 23. These verses talk about having a relationship with the Shepherd. "I shall not want" means that as a disciple of Jesus, God will supply our every need. We can lie down in His perfect rest. When we allow God to lead us by quiet waters our souls find refreshment. He does restore. It is His desire to guide our pathways and to keep us from fearing the evil around us.

I told them that the precious name of Jesus has a purpose. And times of testing enhance our Godly character. He will always be our protection from the evil of this world because God's faithfulness is always available to us without limit to all who believe in Jesus Christ as Lord and Savior. Comfort in its purest form is found in the arms of Jesus. There is hope and abundant blessings when we sit secure at the throne of God's grace.

That evening a dinner was given for our enjoyment, prepared by our gracious host, Sister Grace. I could have stayed there forever with this gentle, loving family of God. Showers of blessings indeed!

Before we left Michigan, the Holy Spirit had told me to bring string for a visual aide. While in prayer for our next meeting, I understood why. The Spirit of God told me how to prepare the string. Naomi and I cut the string into many, many pieces about eight inches long. We folded hundreds of string pieces in half and placed an easy knot in the middle of each one. The Holy Spirit said to give these strings out to each fellowship as directed by the Lord.

One place God directed me to use the string was in Collierville, Tennessee. Ken Toney, Pastor of The Dwelling Place gave free rein for the Spirit of God to lead, and lead He did. I shared my testimony about my struggle with forgiving and the knots that I had been tied in because of unforgiveness. Afterward I gave an invitation for anyone to come forward who wanted God to take away the strings and knots that had bound them for far too long. Almost every seat emptied. The Spirit of God was at work dealing with the children He loves. Hearts were set free. What a mighty move of God as He led those knotted by the world to freedom in His Son!

The last Saturday we were in Tennessee, I spoke at two churches back to back. It was a fast twenty-minute ride between the two churches, something Pastor John Baker and his lovely wife LeAnne do every Saturday. He is the pastor of two West Tennessee Seventh Day Adventist churches and he had invited my team to share with them this particular Saturday.

Naomi taught the children's sermon in front of the whole church body. I was so proud of her as she is not an up-front kind of person. I ministered on the potter's hands. I shared that when we think we are broken and of no use, God steps in and says, I know I can make something beautiful from this. And He does. I shared that we must go through many fires to become the child of God that He desires us to be. Although painful at the time, we do not go through the pain alone for His Word tells us in both Deuteronomy 31:6 and Hebrews 13:5 that He will never leave us nor forsake us. I testified how thankful I was that God had never left me through the very difficult emotional and spiritual challenges I had endured during and after the death of my son Matthew less than one year before.

The family of God is amazing. No matter what nationality or where we are in the world, or in this case the United States, we always have someone to connect with. We fellowshipped with God's family from India, and Kenya (and England of course, since I am British, I cannot leave myself out) as well as from all over the United States. We ate familiar and unfamiliar foods. We heard familiar and unfamiliar words and dialects. We worshipped God together each in our own languages, yet God understood it all. We believe that God delights in the praises of His people. And praise Him we did. All of these people treated us as kin, a very warm and welcoming extended family.

We encountered many beautiful and godly people during our time in Tennessee, people we now consider family not just friends. Angela exhorted us and prayed with us even though we were just building this friendship. Jared kept us on track and focused on the mission ahead. Tina fed us and worshipped God with us even though we had never met her before. Pheba prayed with us and is still helping to carry our burdens through prayer. Diana's music touched our very soul. Casandra treated us like royalty. Pastor John and LeAnne gave of themselves for our comfort. The list goes on and on and on. Our family had expanded. We are loved. And we love back. Like God, His family is unlimited. No matter where we are, God's people are there to love, support and give of themselves. There are no barriers, because God is a barrier breaker.

With a mixture of happiness and sadness, we wrapped up our mission outreach tour and headed home toward Michigan. With the sale of the books and gifts from many new friends and our new family, we had more than enough money to pay for the printing of book two, Come Lean On Me and ongoing costs of our new ministry. God had provided. God had provided money for the second book. God had provided new friends and family. God had provided new ministry partners. God had provided more than we had thought of or asked for. God is amazing. As we drove homeward we found ourselves thanking God in song for all the wonderful things He gave us to enjoy.

Celebration of Life
Alan Reece-Jarman

I have fought a good fight,
I have finished my course,
I have kept the faith:

— 2 Timothy 4:7 (KJV)

COME LEAN ON ME

Chapter Fifteen
HOMEWARD BOUND

Alan called me every night while I was away on outreach asking if I had any prayer requests. He would share about his day. He would end by saying just how much he loved me and how very proud he was of me in following the call God had placed on my life. I was getting excited to be going home and to be able to rest in my darling's arms and share the goodness of God with the man I loved, and with whom I had shared the past 39 years of my life. I had no idea what was waiting for me the very next day.

After driving for six hours and covering some 414 miles, Naomi and I decided to take a hotel for the night. "We are no spring chickens," I told her, "just tired out hens." Then we both laughed. Once in our hotel room I put the moneybag in the drawer between the two beds for safekeeping. We settled down for a much needed sleep that followed quickly. In the morning I was woken up when my cell phone rang.

I thought it might be Alan telling me how his new job was going. Alan was making a career change while I was gone on the mission trip to Tennessee. Instead of driving to Battle Creek each work day, he was now going to drive to Ionia, the opposite direction. I was happy for this new opportunity for him. He was happy and excited too. Alan had worked for the past eight and half years as a substance abuse counselor with A Forever Recovery in Battle Creek, Michigan. He had the favor of God with his co-workers and his clients. Everyone loved Alan. Whenever he could, he led people to the Lord. He even was allowed to baptize the new believers in St. Mary's Lake, which lay behind the treatment center. But he longed for a change. He longed to work in a Christian environment. He was looking forward to starting this new job.

So I was surprised and a bit worried when I heard the man's voice on the other end of the line that turned out to be Alan's new boss. Chris shared with me that Alan had not turned up for work and he was concerned for Alan's well being. This was not like Alan. He was always early. I could hear my heart pounding in my ears. Maybe he is just sick, I told myself.

I told Chris I was not at home, but I would find out what the problem was and call him back. I made several calls to friends but no one was available.

Naomi told me to call her son-in-law Erik. She thought it was his day off and he would run and check on Alan for me. I did call Erik. He was available and willing to go and check on "Uncle Alan" as Naomi's family called him. Erik said he would call me right back. It only takes ten minutes to drive from Naomi's house to my house. That was a long ten-minute wait.

While waiting for Erik to call back, Naomi said, "Let's start praising God." She wanted me to focus on God and not on what might be. She led as I tried to follow. I tried to keep focused on God, but it was difficult. My mind was going a hundred miles an hour trying to figure out why Alan had not gone to the job he had so looked forward to.

What seemed like an eternity later, the phone call came and Erik told me in a very calm voice that Uncle Alan had passed away. My chest went tight. My mouth went dry. My mind screamed for the fourth time, NOOOOOOOOOOOO, NOT AGAIN. We grabbed our clothes and headed for the hotel front desk to check out.

Naomi drove home freeing me to answer my cell phone calls. Erik was a 911 dispatcher and so knew all the right people to call to take care of the situation, but I still had to answer many many questions over the phone that day as we drove home. The medical examiner came to my house. He needed several medical questions answered about my husband. He asked me if Alan had had any recent surgeries or if he was taking any medications. I said Alan was fit and healthy in every way. The medical examiner told me he believed Alan died of a broken heart having lost his son one year ago to the month. Erik had taken care of everything by the time we got home. Naomi stayed with me that night.

At one in the morning I woke up with a scare. In the confusion of the early morning phone call and checking out in a hurry, I had left the moneybag in the hotel room drawer between the two beds. Naomi called the hotel to explain what had happened, but was told the room was now occupied and we would have to wait until the person checked out. She called back again after checkout time only to be told they would call us back if anything was found.

I was convinced the person that occupied the room now had found the moneybag. Oh me of little faith! Later in the day the hotel called to say the moneybag had been found. I called Scott at the funeral home to ask him if it was all right to go get the moneybag before coming to see him about arrangements for Alan. Scott told me to deal with the situation, and he would take care of my husband. We jumped in the car and headed back to Indianapolis. At the hotel the front desk receptionist asked if we could identify the contents of the bag. I was so pleased that I had itemized each check number and name into our ministry account book. After being convinced that it was ours, we were given the moneybag back. Checking the contents, nothing was missing. We breathed a sigh of relief and prayed a prayer of thanksgiving.

Back in Michigan we met with Scott Daniels, our local funeral director. After answering numerous questions, I asked Scott if I could go and spend some time with my husband who was still there pending my return visit. "No," came his reply. "It has been too long and Alan has not been embalmed," Scott said. "I don't want the last memory you have of your wonderful husband to be a bad one." His tenderness toward my painful situation was so very touching. He was thinking only of me.

Rebecca, our daughter, had already spent time with her daddy in the room set aside for farewells. She prayed over him, asking God to give him his life back. She pleaded with God to spare her daddy. Rebecca told God how much she needed her daddy in her life, and then Rebecca waited for God to answer her prayer. God did not answer her prayer the way she wanted or asked. She was saddened and heartbroken.

I had so many wonderful stories to share with Alan on my return home from the mission trip. He had told me that when I returned home he would take me out to dinner and sit listening to the many ways God blessed. Now he would see for himself from Heaven. I found it hard not to be able to touch him one more time and say good-bye. I too had believed that God would raise Alan from the dead. I wanted to tell him these stories in person. I wanted to see the joy on his face and hear that special tone in his voice telling me,

Page 111

"Well done. I am so proud of you." It was not to be. God's plans and God's ways are not our plans and ways, yet He knows best.

I have found it very hard living without him. I didn't realize just how much time he filled in my life. Like the days at the end of summer each year when he would do the final grass cutting and I would rake up millions of fallen brown crusty leaves. I found it easiest to put all the leaves on a very large tarp and then holding it by the corners, like a wedding veil, I would drag it behind me to the dump pile in between the trees.

This day I got it in place and called out for Alan to help me tip it over. Suddenly I realized I was on my own. Alan would no longer be there to help me with anything ever again. I let the tarp fall and came into the house shaking with anger.

I sat at our kitchen table and sobbed and sobbed. I could feel anger rising up within me. I started to shout out to God. I shouted angrily. I shouted loud. "What is the reason to keep going? What is the reason to get up in the morning? What is the reason to wash and get dressed? What is the reason? TELL ME GOD!! I NEED TO KNOW, WHAT IS THE REASON?"

Suddenly I was aware of Someone sitting at the table opposite me. I wiped my eyes and nose on the sleeve of my sweater and looked up to see Jesus looking at me feeling my pain. His beautiful face held such compassion for the pain exploding in my heart. Love was so evident in His eyes and such tenderness evident in His gentle voice. "I am the reason," he said. "What other reason do you need?" And then He was gone.

I cried again, but this time my tears were not of self-pity, but of thankfulness. I was thankful that the son of God loved me so very much that He came and sat with me in my greatest hour of need, reassuring me and giving me hope. I was thankful that I could lean on Him for the days ahead. I was thankful that Jesus would be my husband from this day forward and care for me way beyond my expectations.

I have days where I can stay above water, just, and other days when all I can do is cry. I cry for dreams unfulfilled. I cry for plans made that now need to be eliminated from my mind and heart. I had thirty-nine years and one month with the man I loved, the man who kept me laughing. I cry because I no longer have the man that helped me grow closer to God, the father of my children, the prayer warrior of our family. Now he too was gone. I needed to keep going. Alone? No not alone, God would now be my husband.

I will lean on Him more than ever
until He calls me home.

*In hope of eternal life,
which God, that
cannot lie, promised
before the world began
Not to us, O LORD,
not to us but to your
name be the glory,
because of your love
and faithfulness.*

— Psalm 115:1 (NIV)

COME LEAN ON ME

Chapter Sixteen
TO GOD BE THE GLORY

The weekend of October 20, 2018 was a huge mix of emotions. Before Naomi and I left on our ministry trip we had planned a celebration dinner to launch the first of my three books, Come Walk With Me, and to share all about what God had done on our mission trip during the month of September.

When Alan died, I had to set up a time for his Celebration of Life service. The best time for our family was October 21st. Many people encouraged me to cancel or at least postpone the dinner we had planned for the 20th. I did not think this was a good idea. Both times would be a celebration, although now both would be bittersweet.

Many friends and family attended both celebrations. They worked tirelessly to bring food and set up the venues and make the celebrations special with worship music and testimonies. Old missionary friends from Saipan and Kenya surprised me as they came to show their support for me after the death of Alan. New friends from Tennessee came to support me through this rocky time. Family came from as far away as England. Close friends from Nashville gathered to hold me up and carry me through the weekend

They say that many hands make light work. This was certainly the case that weekend. Friends and family supplied food, decorations for the tables and special music for all to enjoy. Tables were beautifully decorated and fully laden with enough food to feed an army. How grateful I was to these many friends and family who helped make both celebrations special!

My church family at Abundant Life Fellowship worked tirelessly for both celebrations leaving me with nothing to do but greet and talk to the people who attended those celebrations. Cathy Liceaga, true to her servant heart, came bearing containers of food and decorations for the book launching celebration. She and her sister Cheryl decorated the venue, laid out the food and were still there at the end of the evening to help clean up.

My long time friend, Michael Farnum, had kindly offered to be the music man for the evening. He played uplifting praise and worship music to enhance the atmosphere. I could strongly sense the presence of the Holy Spirit that evening. A new friend, David Stroner, played his saxophone. While he was playing "Amazing Grace" and "The Old Rugged Cross" I observed lips mouthing the words in an act of praise to God. His saxophone gave the listener a sweet taste of heaven's angelic melody. A beautiful Christian sister, Kim Lloyd, sang a heart-piercing solo called, "The Only Way Out Is Through." This was so meaningful to me personally because I knew there was no way out. I could only go through the days ahead leaning on God as he led me by His indwelling Spirit. Later that evening Kim's brother, Philip, sang a solo called, "Don't Give Up on Victory." Their young voices gave me hope for our future generation to shine for Jesus. As long as youngsters were learning of God and leaning on Him there would always be victory.

Saturday, the morning of the book launch, I opened my front door to a handsome young man I did not recognize right away. When I realized who he was, I flung my arms around his neck and let my tears fall. There, right in front of me, standing at my front door was one of our closest family friends, John Enyart. He had been base leader of our YWAM base on Saipan and Alan's closest friend during those years. He had driven all the way from Kansas City to give his support to my family and me and to attend Alan's Celebration of Life. Andy Elliott, another longtime friend and staff member from our YWAM, Saipan days flew in from Colorado. He and John Enyart both showed up unexpectedly and completed an awesome weekend of celebration.

Alan's Celebration of Life service was held on Sunday at our home church, Abundant Life Fellowship Ministries, here in Nashville, Michigan. More than one hundred friends and family came together to honor this man of integrity.

Shia, our granddaughter, greeted people at the door and handed out the order of service cards. Alan's picture graced the front cover. I wanted everyone to see his picture and remember what a happy and handsome fellow he was. The brown leather cowboy hat he was wearing made him look so distinguished. The look on his face was one of pure contentment.

Inside the left-hand cover were printed these words.

"Whatever we face,
We're never alone,
For God takes our sorrows,
And makes them His own."

I so needed to remember those words. Also on that page was, **"I have fought the good fight, I have finished the course, I have kept the faith."** (2 Timothy 4:7) These words were a great comfort to me. Although I did not want my husband to be gone, I was thankful that he was a man of faith, a man of integrity. These words encouraged me to remember that he had kept his faith in God.

Back in 1985 when Alan first went with YWAM to Mombasa, Kenya, East Africa, Alan met a man named Jared Okoth. Jared, who is now living and working in the United States, came to Michigan to express his grief at the loss of a close brother in Christ. He shared with tears in his eyes of the brother God had brought into his life so many years ago who had made a great impact in his walk of faith. He loved Alan. Jared was so moved with emotions he was unable to finish his speech. Jared's wife, Angela, sang, "It's All About the Cross." Such a dynamic song, sung with the greatest of emotions, moved many people there by the spirit of God working on their hearts. I am so glad it is all about the cross and not about us.

One of my newest Christian sisters, Cheryl Perrine, shared how she had met Alan at Maranatha Bible and Missionary Conference Center just two months before. She took an instant liking to this funny man with a great sense of humor. It was Cheryl that was Alan's link to his new career. She said he was the only man she knew who was promoted to the highest level before he ever started the job. This had me laughing. Alan had been promoted. I needed to remember that. This would be a good way of thinking when the days grew sad.

While I was in Tennessee on outreach I met a beautiful, funny, godly man, Pastor John Baker. Even though I had only known him for a few short weeks, he and his wife, LeAnne, drove all the way from Tennessee to support me during this difficult time. Pastor John's words of encouragement touched my heart as he shared how he wished he had known Alan personally. He said it seemed that the two of them had the same sense of humor and would have put this gift of laughter to good use for the kingdom of God.

Richard, our oldest son, flew in from England to support the family. He spoke about his daddy being his best friend in the entire world. Richard said his life will forever have a void that no one can fill. Holding back his tears, Richard shared that his father was a man after God's own heart. He reminisced that while we lived on Saipan, his daddy would occasionally come into his school and take the morning chapel service. Even as a high school student, he had been proud of his father's stance as a Christian man.

I so appreciated hearing the depth of respect and love that my son held for his father. I was and am thankful that over his lifetime Alan always made a point of reinforcing to his children how much he loved them and cared for them. I was and am thankful that our children knew this. And I was glad to hear them talk about his love now. I knew that Alan's love and values would be carried on in his children. I was thankful that I could look at them and remember Alan's love and laughter and his Christian values.

My heart broke as our granddaughter Shia shared the emptiness she now felt, first with the passing of her uncle Matt, then just a year later, with the passing of her papa. I knew that I would not be able to fill that emptiness. I was thankful, however, that she had the first 18 years of her life with them and that she would have sweet and happy memories to cherish forever. I was grateful that her papa had told her repeatedly just how much he loved her. I was glad that he had prayed for her every day. I was glad that he had spoken into her life just how important it is to have a life filled with God.

I listened as Shia's mum, our daughter Rebecca, spoke through a shattered heart. It had only been one year since her brother had gone to glory. Her daddy's passing was another hard hit, but she kept her speech positive and humorous. I was so proud of her, for I could see and hear how much it took out of her emotionally. I listened as Rebecca shared about the nonsense code words she and her daddy spoke when they were interacting with each other and just for a second I saw a twinkle in her eye as she jumped back in time to when they had used such words. When she was finished, she walked over to the front row where I was sitting with Shia and pulled us both up into a deep heartfelt family hug that we all needed.

My pastor, the reverend Dr. David R. MacDonald spoke about what it is to be a Christian. He explained clearly how to become one and gave an open invitation for anyone who wanted to receive Christ as their personal savior. Hands were raised high to acknowledge their need of a savior. Alan would have loved to see that even in his passing, his life was being used to further the kingdom of God. This day, a celebration of a wonderful life, totally honored God.

I know that when it's time for me to be "homeward bound," I will see my loved ones again. I need to say each morning, "Thank you, God, for a new day to serve You; and live expecting, waiting and believing for the return of my Lord and my Savior, JESUS CHRIST."

For those of you who want to know more about God or how to make Him Lord and Savior of your life, just follow these few simple steps. Admit you are a sinner. Believe in your heart that God raised Jesus (His son) from the dead. Confess with your mouth that Jesus Christ is Lord and you will be saved. It is not a formula. It is a heart change.

There is no wrong way to ask God to be Lord of your life. Just talk to Him. He understands every tongue of every nation on earth. He is waiting just for you. You matter to God. Let Him show you just how much. Do not put it off. You are not guaranteed another day. Act now!

A B C's of Salvation

A - Admit you are a sinner. We are all sinners by nature and by choice.
Romans 3:23 *For all have sinned and come short of the glory of God.*

B - Believe you can receive eternal life as a free gift.
Romans 6:23 *For the wages of sin is death but the (free) gift of God is eternal life through Jesus Christ our Lord.*

C - Confess and Come to Christ.
Romans 10:9 *If you confess with your mouth that Jesus Christ is Lord, believe in your heart that God raised Him from the dead, you shall be saved.*

If you make a decision for Christ please contact me. It will encourage my heart. If you have any questions about Christ or Christianity please contact me. I will try my best to answer your questions. Please use this e-mail address: hopeministries017@gmail.com

Every blessing, Ellen

ACKNOWLEDGEMENTS

I thank God for my family and friends who have stood with me over the past year and a half or so. It has been a hard time. They have helped me not lose my way. They have called me; some daily, to make sure I am ok. They have supplied me with food, kept my driveway plowed and encouraged me in the things of God. I am eternally grateful. As much as I would like to mention everyone who has entered my life in these last 18 or so months there are too many to list in this book. I apologize if I offend anyone by leaving his or her name out. It is not my intention.

Here are a few of the many people that I feel need to be acknowledged. First and foremost my late husband, Alan, who loved me with all of his heart and encouraged me to follow God's prompting to write my books and share them with the world. I am eternally thankful for my children: Dee, Richie, Bexs and Matt. Their encouragement keeps me going. I thank my granddaughters, Shia for always being positive and for going out of her way to spend part of her weekends with me so I do not have to be alone so much, and Jaysona-Skye for always being positive and full of life.

I send out an immense heartfelt thank you to the following friends who worked so very tirelessly to help make my book, Come Walk With Me, and its dinner celebration a huge success: my church family at Abundant Life Fellowship Ministries for their unending support, Cathy & Cheryl for their servant hearts, Mike Farnum - our talented and gifted DJ, David Stroner saxophonist extraordinaire, and for Kim Lloyd and Philip Morris whose angelic voices lifted my tired spirit.

I am beyond grateful to all of the people who made Alan's Celebration Of Life Service a splendid homegoing memorial.   Once again I am deeply indebted to my family at Abundant Life Fellowship Ministries who have stayed with me through thick and thin. I am so grateful that once a brother or sister in Christ always a brother or sister in Christ. It does not matter how many years pass; Jared, John, and Andy, you are still my brothers. Angela, Pastor John, LeAnne and Cheryl; I am so glad you are my new family in Christ.

There is no distance or limits to the family of God. The welcome of the saints regardless of location is always warm and inviting. I am thankful for this warm invitation on all of our stops on our mission trip.

Apostle Anna Shears and your church family, Temple of Light Global Church, thank you for treating me like royalty in opening your hearts and homes for my comfort.

Tina Herron, you make the most amazing meals. You give the biggest hugs and warmest smiles and make me feel like I have known you forever.

Pastor Babu Thomas and Sister Grace, my beautiful Indian family, your home smelled delectable as I entered through the door. I found it hard to concentrate on my sermon with those smells wafting up into my nose. I am humbled that you allowed me the privilege of sharing God's word to your flock. Next time we meet I hope to know at least one word in your native tongue.

Pastor Ken Toney and The Dwelling Place family, thank you for giving me free rein to allow the Holy Spirit to move as I ministered. I am blessed beyond words that you allowed me, a stranger, to give my testimony of the presence and power of God throughout my life.

Dr. Santosh and Pheba Abraham, (Joshua and Caleb, too) thank you for the incredible feast I enjoyed at Union University. Sitting around the table and chatting gave me a small taste of what I believe it will be like in Heaven when we sit around His banqueting table with all the brothers and sisters from all nations.

Casandra Berry, your smile, your thoughtfulness, and generous giving is a true example of a disciple of Christ. Thank you for accepting me as your sister.

Pastor Charles Robinson, thank you for trusting God and honoring the Holy Spirit's direction in your kind invitation to allow me to speak to your church family, Devout Temple, Holiness Church. What a fine group of believers you are.

I want to express a special word of appreciation to: Pastor Debbie Moore, thank you so much for your willingness to proofread this book. (And my first book, too)   Thank you for the countless hours of backache and eye strain you endured on my behalf correcting all the tons of grammar mistakes and helping this book make sense to the reader. I love you my sister.

Last but not least, a super-dooper heart load of thanks to my ministry partner, Naomi. Without her patience, help, and support (and slave driving) this book would still be in its infancy.

But mostly, I give my unbounded thanks to God, who found me worthy to carry His light of love, peace, hope and inner healing to this lost and hurting world.

Previous books
by Ellen Reece-Jarman

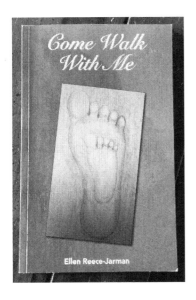

Coming soon:

Come Learn From Me –

Devotional with a twist